I0558171

# GURDJIEFF AND KUNDABUFFER

—⁓—

## FOOD FOR THE MOON

by R Bloor

**KARNAK PRESS**

**KARNAK PRESS**
Austin, Texas

## Gurdjieff and Kundabuffer
### Food For The Moon

Copyright © 2023 by Robin Bloor

ISBN 978-1-957278-07-0

Printed in the United States of America

# Gurdjieff
# and
# Kundabuffer

## Food For The Moon

**George Ivanovic Gurdjieff**

*"There are no people in The Work, only places."*

*~ Rina Hands*

# Contents

# Gurdjieff and Kundabuffer

# CHAPTER I

# Introduction

*"In right knowledge the study of man must proceed on parallel lines with the study of the world, and the study of the world must run parallel with the study of man."*
*~ G Gurdjieff*

Perhaps the most surprising idea Gurdjieff introduced when he brought The Work to the West was that organic life on Earth, including humanity itself, feeds the Moon. From a conventional perspective, this is an outlandish idea. Gurdjieff clearly knew that many people would find it incomprehensible and reject it outright. Many of the psychological ideas of The Work are almost self-evident, and those that are not are much easier to accept than the idea of our feeding the Moon".

However, The Work is not confined to psychology. In introducing The Work to his Russian groups and later to groups in Europe and America, Gurdjieff described the cosmology of The Work in detail, with "the basics"– the Law of Three, the Octave, and the Ray of Creation – at the forefront. He also stated plainly that the study of The Work required the examination of both the inner and external worlds.

Thus, Gurdjieff's Objective Science, with all its trappings, is the prism through which we need to try to understand the external world. When it comes to the visible components of the Ray of Creation – Galaxies, the Sun, the Planets, the Earth, and the Moon – the theory is easy to accept. It seems to accord to some degree with established astronomical knowledge.

When it comes to the Side Octave from the Sun and organic life on Earth, however, it is less clear. The astrological implications – that the movements of Planets directly influence life on Earth – are familiar from the perspective of astrology and not too difficult to accept, but the idea of feeding the Moon strains credibility.

It would perhaps be less bewildering if *Beelzebub's Tales* were not so insistent on this point and didn't also declare that Man not only feeds the Moon, but that the Universe ensures that he does so without complaint by means of a specific organ – the organ Kundabuffer – which was once implanted in Man by higher beings to ensure just that.

Kundabuffer is not mentioned by name in Peter Ouspensky's *In Search of the Miraculous*, and there is little focus on that idea. Perhaps as a consequence, some people in The Work do not take the text of *Beelzebub's Tales* literally where it discusses Kundabuffer – preferring to believe that Kundabuffer is some kind of obscure metaphor that Gurdjieff invented.

That was indeed an idea that I entertained on my first reading of Gurdjieff's masterpiece. But the more times I read the book, the less plausible this metaphor explanation seemed.

*The Tales* plainly states many times that mankind's situation – our situation – can be attributed to two distinct causes:

1. The consequences of the properties of the organ Kundabuffer.

2. The abnormal conditions of ordinary being-existence which humanity itself gradually established.

This book examines that proposition.

# CHAPTER II

## Early Traces of Kundabuffer

*"In every man there has been implanted a need for knowledge, differing only in its intensity."*
*~ Gurdjieff*

The beguiling phrase "the consequences of the properties of the organ Kundabuffer" occurs fifty-four times in *The Tales*. It is a constant drumbeat, the rhythm of which enters the mind of the reader. However, nowhere in *The Tales* does Gurdjieff explain precisely what he means by those words.

Happily, *The Tales* is not the only place where he mentioned the topic. He touched on it in three separate lectures, all of which he gave years before he authored *The Tales*. Indeed he gave the first of these lectures before he established his institute in France.

The notes from the lecture read as follows:

**LECTURE (PRE-INSTITUTE)**

*So is the ordinary man. He can live all his life as he is.*

*At the same time Nature has given him the possibility of changing, but this does not mean that any change will necessarily take place.*

*This change you speak of is possible, but it is difficult to say if anyone has the chance of reaching it. There are many reasons not dependent on us, which may prevent this.*

*The chief reason is in ourselves, and it is the Kundabuffer as it is called.*

*To understand clearly what this new thing is, we must stop here and go into further details. Nature in her foresight has given to man's machine a certain property, which protects the man from feeling and sensing reality.*

*That is the Kundabuffer.*

*Let us take a real fact. All men are mortal and every man can die at any moment. I can imagine that Mr. Smith comes out from the theater, and crossing the street, he falls under an automobile which crushes him to death. Or a signboard is torn off and falls just on the head of Mr. Jones and kills him on the spot. Or Mr. Brown eats crayfish, poisons himself, and dies the next day without anyone being able to save him.*

*All this, everybody can easily imagine. But, we ask, can anyone imagine that he himself this moment or tomorrow, or in one year or in ten years will also die? Really if we think of this carefully – death is a terror. What is more terrible than death? What would happen if he really imagined this terror, his own death? Can you imagine the terror?*

*You cannot imagine your own death, but you can imagine the death of another. Besides these terrors there are many other terrors in reality, which we do not realize, which we do not see. If men realized them they would hang themselves from terror. But nobody sees this. Why? Perhaps somebody will say it is our will which protects us from realizing these terrors? But then why does not our will protect us from small fears?*

*Imagine you come home, undress, go to bed, and at the same moment that you cover yourself with the blanket something jumps from under the bed, runs across your body and hides itself in the folds of the blanket. You throw off your blanket, draw up your feet and see a mouse. Imagine this picture, and almost from thinking about it – a shiver will run through your body. And what was so terrifying, in this, a house mouse, the most harmless of beasts. You don't feel terror before inevitable deaths but you are afraid of a mouse, are afraid of a thousand trifles which may only possibly occur.*

*These terrors on account of which you will not hang yourself are* admitted by Nature as offensive for your existence, to the extent in which they are necessary to give you the experiences of joy and sorrow, pleasure and pain. Without them, there could not exist the experiences of which our life is made up. This is the source of the many troubles, griefs, efforts, self-loves, vanities which force man to act, to attain, and have illusions and disillusions. That is what supports life.

These same things give us dreams, imaginations, and illusions, and awake the most various wishes in man. And he is always full of them. They give him the necessary impulse and fill his life, and he has no time to feel reality. Often those aims are inaccessible, but man does not see this and keeps on trying and trying. When one kind of trouble passes – another appears. Man's machine has to work all the time.

And now imagine that you know, that you remember, if only with your head, that you have in one month to die. Exactly in one month. What will remain then of all that has filled our day? Everything that you have will lose its meaning and will count as nothing. And the newspaper with your morning coffee, and the polite greeting from your neighbors on the stairs, your professional work and belongings, and theater in the evening, and rest and sleep – to what purpose is all this?

But if death will come only in a year or two? Even then, everything will no longer have the same meaning that it had for us before.

Involuntarily you ask: if that is so, why should we live?

Just not because your life is for yourself. Your life is necessary to somebody else, who watches over it and takes care of it, that you may be able to live a little better. We take and we watch over the lives of our sheep and pigs. When we feed them, do we do this because we care about them, or for the sake of their lives? No, we make their lives happy and good, and arrange for them all sorts of comforts in order that when the time comes to kill them, we may have better meat and more fat.

Just in the same way, evidently, somebody wants us to live, wants us not to see all our terrors and not to hang ourselves but wants us to live long, so that the one to whom we are necessary will gently and softly kill us when the time comes. Not to see reality and not to feel it as it is, is the main form of our slavery. We have many slaveries, *but this one is the first, is the chief one. That is the law of Nature. The existence of the whole of humanity and of all that lives is indispensable to the great ones. In life there is a great aim, and this justifies her destiny. We have to serve as slaves – that is our destiny. And at the same time, Nature has foreseen the possibility, but not for everyone, to throw off this slavery.*

*This throwing-off is the first liberation. Life has two directions, life is like two rivers.*

*All living beings on earth are subdivided into two currents; some flow with one current, the others with the other. The one part are subordinate and have in themselves one kind of law, the others another. The two laws always come into collision, one with the other, cross each other, run side by side, never mixing, supporting each other; necessary, one to the other. Always it was so, always it will be so. Now if we take the life of the masses, their life as a whole is like one of the rivers, in which each drop of water represents the life of an individual man or of some living creature.*

*All these separate drops go to make up the river, which in its turn is a link in the cosmic chain. The current of this river flows according to general cosmic law. All its turnings, all its curves, all its changes have a quite a definite destination. For this destination each drop plays only in as much as it is a particle of the big river.*

*The law does not extend itself to the separate drops. The changing of place of the drops, their direction, their movement, have only a casual character. Now the drop is here, in one moment there. One moment it is on the surface, another it sinks. Occasionally it collides with another, sinks. Or it flows quickly or slowly, whether it is good or bad depends on the place where it falls.*

*It has no separate laws. It has no personal fate. Fate is only for the whole river; all the drops have this. Personal grief, joy, happiness, suffering, all are accidentally in this current.*

*But each drop has a principal possibility of leaving this common current and jumping into the neighboring second river. That is also a law of Nature.*

*For this, the drop has to know how to use the inertia of the whole river; how to use the occasional shocks to come to the surface and nearer to the banks from which it is easier to jump.*

It is necessary to choose the place and the time. It is necessary to make use of the wind, of the current of the storms, if such occurs. Then the drop has a chance with the spray to rise and jump into the neighboring river.

From the moment of getting there, it is in another life and therefore subject to other laws.

In this river, there are laws for the separate drops. There is the law of turn. When the drop rises or sinks to the bottom, it is not accidental, but according to a certain law. This law is also mechanical as in the first river. Coming to the surface, the drop gets heavier and sinks. In the depths it loses weight and rises. To flow on the surface is good for it, but to be in the depths is evil. And here much depends on knowledge and effort.

This river has many little streams. It is necessary to get into the right stream and to remain on the surface as long as possible in order to gain the possibility of reaching another bed, and so on. We are now in the first river. Until we are passive we shall be driven about and exposed to all accidents. We are slaves of these accidents. At the same time however, Nature has given us permission to be able to get away from this slavery. And so when one speaks of "liberation," it means just the getting into another river.

But this is certainly not so simple, to "want to pass and you pass." It is necessary to make a long preparation, a very strong wish is necessary. It is necessary to renounce all the blessings of the world that are in the first river. For this, it is necessary to die for this river. Just about this death it is spoken in all religions. If you do not die you will not be resurrected. This is not spoken about the death of the physical body. For such death it is not necessary to be resurrected. If there is soul, moreover, an immortal soul, it can do without this body, the loss of which is called death.

And the cause of the resurrection is not to appear before God, as we are taught by the contemporary fathers of the Church. No, Christ and all others spoke about death which can occur even while we are in life, about the death of the tyrant from whom comes our slavery, and upon whose death depends the first chief liberation of man. What I am about to tell may appear at the first glance to be the delirium of a madman. For some it will remain so. Nevertheless I will tell. And at the same time, according to my ideas, I reckon it a *big sin to speak of it. If I have sinned against Nature, my chief sin will be reckoned in this, about which I am going to speak.*

*All wars, all disputes, all misunderstandings, all misfortunes, all experiences which seem terrible when they occur, when they have passed we can see are not worth a half-penny. In this sense, as if from a fly one should get an elephant, and now from an elephant a fly. The reason for this is always the same property of the man, that he reflects reality in the reverse.*

*During such events, all are slaves, and all are under a general hypnosis. Where is the dignity attributed to man? Where is man with his free will?*

*It was always so and it will be always so with the masses, because if there will not be slaves, there will not be masters, there will not be life.*

*But at the same time, to some men it is given to get out from beneath the mass hypnosis. Men so little realize this mass hypnosis, that the one who is more or less free from it, appears as a being of a lower order.*

*That which is called bravery in war is really only a manifestation of this mass hypnosis. There exist whole nations which reckon the others cowards, as for example, the Russians the Jews. But the Jewish drummer who, according to the understanding of the Russians, out of cowardice hides in a ditch during the battle, is really a more normal man, more free than they are. That which he has is personal, while for the others, everything personal is missing. There remains only the mass hypnosis. He is the slave only of his personal qualities, while they are twice slaves.*

*If we take from a man all his illusions, all that prevents him from seeing the true reality – that is, all his interests, his agitations, his awakenings, his hopes; with them disappear all his aspirations. Everything will be empty. All the impulses of his psyche will be stopped. There will remain an empty being, an empty body which will live only physiologically. That is the death of the "I." The death of everything of which it consisted, the destruction of everything false, accumulated through ignorance and lack of experience.*

*All that will remain in him will be there only as material, not as he himself. Only then will it be possible, if there is strength enough, to collect a new material, and that only by choice. Then man himself takes, and it is not as formerly when something was put into him according to what something else wanted. It is "difficult," but this word is not adequate. The word "impossible" is also bad, because in principle it is possible, although it is a thousand times more difficult than from nothing to become through honest work a millionaire.*[1]

The second mention of Kundabuffer can be found in the Q & A session at the end of a lecture given on March 1st in New York in 1924. It reads as follows:

### [In answer to a question about the moon.]

*The moon is man's big enemy. We serve the moon. Last time you heard about Kundabuffer. Kundabuffer is the moon's representative on earth. We are like the moon's sheep, which it cleans, feeds and shears, and keeps for its own purposes. But when it is hungry it kills a lot of them. All organic life works for the moon. Passive man serves involution; and active man, evolution. You must choose. But there is a principle: in one service you can hope for a career; in the other you receive much but without a career. In both cases we are slaves, for in both cases we have a master. Inside us we also have a moon, a sun and so on. We are a whole system. If you know what your moon is and does, you can understand the cosmos.*[2]

The final mention of Kundabuffer is found in the notes of a lecture given later in 1924, in Chicago.

### LECTURE, CHICAGO 1924

*Kundabuffer at base of spine, prevents our seeing things as they are. If we saw ourselves as we really are, we would hang ourselves. Man must desire a way with his essence – he is really afraid to ask himself if he really wants a way. He may want the way very much with his mind, but when work begins he finds he never even thought of wanting it.*

*When emotion positive, must also be negative. Transcend both to be free. Strong belief in one direction means strong belief in opposite. At Institute, suffering adjusted and divided between centers. Conscience is man's particularity.*

---

[1] *Gurdjieff's Early Talks 1914 - 1931, p36*
[2] *Gurdjieff's Early Talks 1914 - 1931, p367*

*We often know others far better than ourselves, therefore mutual help is very profitable. One-centered activity is hallucination – two-center activity is semi-hallucination – three-center is none.*

*Scientific classification, vertebrate and non-vertebrate. Gurdjieff's by number of brains. Many animals have same number of brains as man – who happens to be a kind of animal by chance; other animals by law of adaptation, and with the necessary environments may become like man. Man has many brains, some of which have the property of cosmic consciousness, others of instinctive mechanical consciousness. Formulatory apparatus is of latter kind. Therefore, our thinking must be mechanical.*

*In process of ages, owing to wrong education, etc., formulatory apparatus usurped function of real mental center. It was originally to collect impressions. Thoughts in formulatory apparatus always change. What we have in other centers always remains. It is ours. Aim of all ways the same. At the end of Yogi training, begin Monk's, then Fakir's, and vice versa. Fourth Way, Haida Way, to study all one can know. It differs from other ways by being much quicker and therefore more difficult. Three center development simultaneously. Astral body not immortal, mechanical like our body but finer. From it, mental body can be developed, then divine body, and only then can one begin to develop immortal soul and only then is reincarnation possible. Possessor of astral body dies, when astral body disintegrates. Same with has immortal soul mental body and physical body. He who never dies.*

*In talking, formulatory apparatus talks to formulatory apparatus. Vibrations of former received in latter. If message felt in speaking, then felt by other in emotional center. All is vibration. Sin in ignorance not so serious as sin knowing it is wrong. All actions produce vibrations which produce some result. We must suffer for our sins before we can begin real development. Impartial judgment only possible when inwardly free. One center acceptance never criticizes, we do when one center questions impression of other. Formulatory apparatus has no inherent energy, robs it from other centers. Everything is impressed on brains. Experiments have been made with newly born children. Action in one center reacts on others, in all parts of the body, even to points outside the body. Man's intelligence varies in proportion to his capacity to prevent these fluctua-*

*tions passing from one center to another.*[3]

There is also a mention of Kundalini from the same source. It appears among a list of sayings and proclaims:

> *Kundalini at base of spine prevents our seeing things as they are; it is the representative of the moon; it is necessary for life, for if we saw things as they were we'd hang ourselves.*[4]

## From *In Search of the Miraculous*

The topic of Kundabuffer is briefly discussed in *In Search of the Miraculous*. Gurdjieff introduces the topic by recounting the Parable of the Magician, which he says originates in the East. The story is as follows:

A Magician owned a large flock of sheep. However, the sheep were difficult to manage and troublesome. They realized that the Magician kept them just to shear them for wool and slaughter them for meat. They constantly tried to escape, wandering off over the hills and into the forest, some falling into ravines and others gaining their freedom. The Magician did not want to pay the cost of hiring shepherds and surrounding his pastures with barbed wire. So, he pondered the problem and devised a solution.

He hypnotized the sheep, planting cunning suggestions in their subconscious. He suggested three things:

- Firstly, he told them that they were immortal, and that no harm was done to them when they were skinned and slaughtered. Indeed, it was good for them and also a pleasant experience.

- Secondly, he suggested to them that, if something were going to happen to them, it would not happen today or even soon, so they had no need to be concerned about it.

- Thirdly, he told them that they were not sheep at all. He told some that they were lions, others that they were eagles, and he

---

[3] *Gurdjieff's Early Talks 1914 - 1931, p388*
[4] *Gurdjieff's Early Talks 1914 - 1931, p425*

told some that they were men, and he even told some of them that they were magicians.

As a consequence, his problem vanished away.

Gurdjieff claimed that this tale provided a good illustration of humanity's position. Man is farmed, and he has no idea of this. He should fear his own death, but he does not. People's minds have been filled with various "comforting" myths about what happens at death. None of these myths suggest that you become food for something else.

In connection with this parable, he also spoke about Kundalini, which he equated to Kundabuffer, noting that occult literature was dangerously misleading about it. The "serpent of Kundalini" is often described as a mystical power residing at the base of the spine that can be awakened to deliver great benefit. Kundalini, he asserted, was neither desirable nor useful. He said it represented the power of imagination and fantasy, which often takes the place of real functions. When a man imagines that he has special powers, this is simply Kundalini in action. Kundalini can act in all centers, and with its help, all the centers can be satisfied with the imaginary instead of the real.

## In Summary

If we thread all of this information together we arrive at the following picture:

- Kundabuffer is implanted by in man Nature. It protects man from feeling and sensing reality.

- The implication from this collection of lecture notes is that it is implanted in every man or woman soon after conception.

- Because of Kundabuffer we cannot imagine our own death, even though we can imagine the death of another. If men clearly saw their true situation they would hang themselves out of terror.

– Because of Kundabuffer we are prey only to "very small fears."
The small fears are allowed by nature. They form the basis of
our joys and sorrows, our pleasure and pain. They are the very
fabric of a normal man's life.

– Kundabuffer implanted by Nature acts as the moon's representative on earth. We are like the moon's sheep, which it
cleans, feeds, shears, and ultimately kills for food. Kundabuffer
hypnotized us. We are slaves to Nature and the effects of Kundabuffer are the chains that enslave us.

– All organic life on earth works for the moon and feeds the
moon. Nature provides the possibility to escape this slavery –
but only to man, and then only to a few men.

GURDJIEFF AND KUNDABUFFER

# CHAPTER III

# The Allegories

*"A myth is far truer than a history, for a history only gives a story of the shadows, whereas a myth gives a story of the substances that cast the shadows."*

~ *Annie Besant*

Gurdjieff titled his series of books "ALL and Everything," implying that these books encompassed all his teachings. This title, prominently displayed on the cover of the first series, as in the adjacent illustration, carries a deeper significance.

In *The Tales*, Gurdjieff capitalized words relating to the Absolute, in line with the usual practice in sacred books - a practice known as "reverential capitalization." So the capitalization of "ALL" in "All and Everything" suggests this interpretation: "ALL" refers to the Absolute, the creator. On the other hand, "Everything" implies

*Figure 1. The Original Cover*

the vastness of creation, from galaxies to atoms, and everything in between. It conveys the idea that Gurdjieff's three series of books encompass all that humanity can know.

The three books of the First Series, have two titles: *An Objectively Impartial Criticism of the Life of Man* and *Beelzebub's Tales to His Grandson.* This is not a title and a subtitle, it is two alternative titles. Publishers have nearly always used the latter title on the cover of the book. But Gurdjieff placed the former title first. When referring to the book directly, in other writings, Gurdjieff tended to use only that first title. When Gurdjieff refers to the book directly in the text of *The Tales* which he does only once, he uses just the first of the two titles. The text reads as follows:

> *"For example, an ordinary good fellow with a character of, as they say, one of 'God's angels,' suddenly became as irritable as those of whom our dear Mullah Nassr Eddin once said:*

> *"'He is as irritable as a man who has just undergone full treatment by a famous European nerve specialist.'*

> *"Or again, beings who one day had been as pacific as the little butter 'lambs' which the pious place on the festal table at their most important religious feasts, would on the next day get as exasperated as a German professor when some Frenchman, also a professor, discovers something new in contemporary science.*

> *"Or again, a being whose love resembled that of a contemporary terrestrial suitor for a rich widow – of course before he has received a single penny from her – would turn just as spiteful as one of those malicious persons who, foaming at the mouth, will hate that poor author who is now writing about you and me, in his work entitled An Objectively Impartial Criticism of the Life of Man.*[5]

The only other time he refers to the book, in *Life Is Real Only Then, When 'I Am',* it is the same. He writes:

> *This benevolent advice of mine to you Americans, composing in the given case this group, and who became, thanks to a series of accidentally arranged circumstances of life, my nearest essential friends, consists in indicating the categorical necessity that each of*

---

[5] *The Tales, Ch XLII. Beelzebub in America, p972-973*

*you should cease entirely, at least for three months, the reading of your newspapers and magazines, and during this time should become as well acquainted as possible with the contents of all three books of the first series of my writings entitled An Objectively Impartial Criticism of the Life of Man.*[6]

The primary title, *An Objectively Impartial Criticism of the Life of Man*, is our focus in this book as we differentiate between the human behavior Beelzebub describes as the fault of Man and human behavior resulting from the consequences of the properties of Kundabuffer.

## The Allegorical Nature of *The Tales*

*The Tales* can be viewed as a series of allegories, in the sense that All of Beelzebub's tales have both a literal and a metaphorical meaning. Gurdjieff provides a simple illustration of allegory in *The Tales* when he describes the allegorical statue of the Akhaldan Society that he encountered in Samlios.

> *"The statue I saw in the city of Samlios and which greatly interested me, was the emblem of this society, and was called 'Conscience.'*

> *"It represented an allegorical being, each part of whose planetary body was composed of a part of the planetary body of some definite form of being existing there, but of the parts of those beings of other forms who, according to the crystallized notions of the three-brained beings there, had to perfection one or another being-function.*

> *"The main mass of the planetary body of the said allegorical being was represented by the trunk of a being there of definite form, called 'Bull.'*

> *"This Bull trunk rested on the four legs of another being existing there, also of a definite form, called 'Lion,' and to that part of the Bull trunk called its 'back' two large wings were attached similar in appearance to those of a strong bird-being breeding there, called 'Eagle.'*

> *"And on the place where the head should be, there was fixed to the Bull trunk, by means of a piece of 'amber,' two breasts representing*

---

[6] *Life Is Real Only Then, When 'I Am', p103*

*in themselves what are called 'Breasts of a virgin.'*

"When I became interested on the continent Atlantis in this strange allegorical image, and then enquired about its meaning, one of the learned members of the Great Society of men-beings explained it to me as follows:

"'This allegorical figure is the emblem of the society Akhaldan and serves for all its members as a stimulus constantly to recall and awaken in them the corresponding impulses attributed to this allegorical figure.'

"Further he continued:

"'Each part of this allegorical figure gives to every member of our society in all the three independently associating parts of his common presence, namely, in the body, in the thoughts, and in the feelings, a shock for corresponding associations for those separate cognizances which in their totality can alone give us the possibility of gradually getting rid of those undesirable factors present in every one of us, both those transmitted to us by heredity as well as those acquired by ourselves personally, which gradually engender within us impulses undesirable for us, and as a consequence of which we are not as we might be. [7]

It is also written from Gurdjieff's perspective. This is not at all clear to the first time reader, who usually finds the book to be confusing and obscure. For example, the term "cosmic unit" occurs ten times in *The Tales,* without any explanation as to what it means. Almost certainly the reader does not know. A cosmic unit is a living being. Gurdjieff also uses the words "arisings" and "beings" to denote life forms. To align with Gurdjieff's perspective and the text of *The Tales,* you must discard the world-view that was educated into you.

Our typical "world view" is atheistic. It asserts that only biological entities from bacteria to man are living things and everything else, no matter how large or small is not alive.

*The Tales* asserts otherwise. The universe is alive; galaxies are alive; stars, from red giants to brown dwarfs, are alive; planets and moons are alive; there is an invisible realm of angels and archangels that are

---

[7] *The Tales, Ch XXIII, Beelzebub's Fourth Sojourn On The Earth, p308-309*

very much alive; the whole spectrum of biological life from man to microbe is alive; viruses are alive; atoms are alive; electrons are alive. All are cosmic units or cosmoses. We not only adopt that perspective, but the view that all living things are alive in a similar way. As Gurdjieff put it, "God, Man and microbe are the same system."

From this perspective there are only two classifications of things in the Universe: living beings at every scale and substances which are being transformed as part of some process within a living being. Think of an item of food - for example a chicken leg. It is not a living being even though it was once part of one. It is a collection of substances some of which can be food for man. When a man eats a chicken leg the substances within it are broken down and digested and they again become part of a living being.

All substances without exception are involved in some kind of circulation - being processed by living beings in some way. The Universe comprises a vast circulation of substances through the beings that process them. This is referred to in general as the Trogoautoegocratic process.

One way to study this world is by means of The Ray of Creation, the octave that begins with the Absolute (as *Do*) and descends to the Moon (*Re*). This is described in detail in *In Search of the Miraculous* by Ouspensky.[8] At the macro scale, it represents the whole universe. However there is also a corresponding Ray of Creation in Man – which implies that there is something that corresponds to the Absolute in man, something that corresponds to the Sun, and the Planets and the Earth and the Moon. And of course, there are circulations of substances.

This is so for all beings at every level.

We can also represent beings (cosmic units) using the enneagram. The enneagram provides a more complete representation of a being than the Ray of Creation – as it can be used to depict the three oc-

---

[8] *In Search of the Miraculous by Peter Ouspensky, from Chapter V onwards*

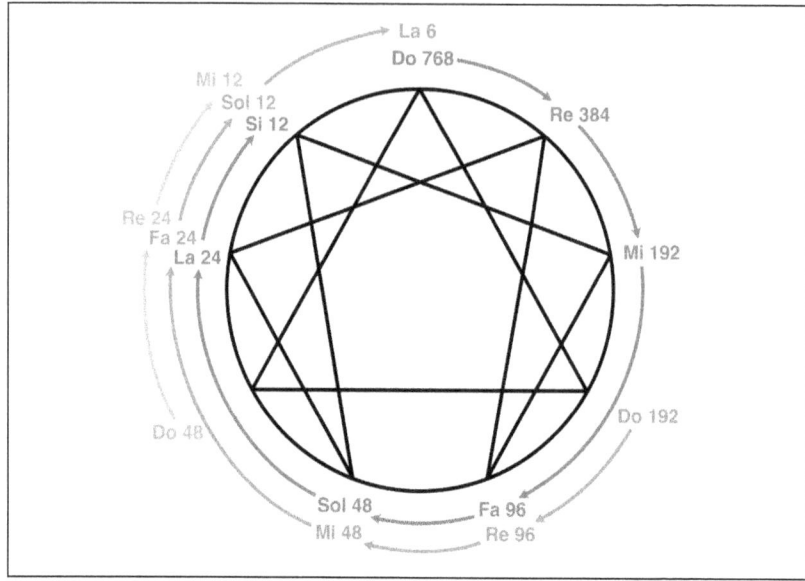

*Figure 2. The Enneagram of a Three Brained Being*

taves of food that determine the physical and psychic structure of the being. Not all beings are the same in this respect.

In *In Search of the Miraculous* Gurdjieff is quoted by Ouspensky as follows:

> *"Each completed whole, each cosmos, each organism, each plant, is an enneagram," he said. "But not each of these enneagrams has an inner triangle. The inner triangle stands for the presence of higher elements, according to the scale of 'hydrogens,' in a given organism."*[9]

So if we look at *Figure 2* on the previous page, the enneagram shown represents a being, like man, whose enneagram possesses an inner triangle. An octave begins at each of the vertices of the inner triangle. The octave of normal food at the apex of the triangle (*Do 768*), the octave of air at the next vertex (*Do 192*) and the octave of impressions at the third vertex (*Do 48*).

Irrespective of whether their enneagrams include an inner triangle, biological beings all consume three foods: they eat, breath and per-

---

[9] *In Search of the Miraculous* by Peter Ouspensky, p293

ceive in some way. Nevertheless, it is not immediately clear how a planet, a volcano or an archangel eats, breathes and perceives.

## The Unique Subjective

Another characteristic of beings is that, with the exception of the Absolute himself and beings at the level of the Sun Absolute, all beings are mortal, and experience a particular lifetime. For man, it is 70-80 years; for horses 25-30 years; for butterflies it can be less than two months. For planets and suns we cannot know for sure. They exist on a different scale to biological beings.

In *The Tales* Gurdjieff characterizes time as "the unique subjective" asserting that even though some creatures live much shorter lives, if measured in (years and days), subjectively their experience of their lifetime time is equivalent to that of man. Beelzebub says:

> "In order that you may meanwhile represent to yourself, if only approximately, what I have just said, let us take as an example the process of the flow of Time proceeding in any drop of the water in that decanter standing there on the table.

> "Every drop of water in that decanter is in itself also a whole independent world, a world of 'Microcosmoses.'

> "In that little world, as in other cosmoses, there also arise and exist relatively independent infinitesimal 'individuals' or 'beings.'

> "For the beings of that infinitesimal world also, Time flows in the same sequence in which the flow of Time is sensed by all individuals in all other cosmoses. These infinitesimal beings also, like the beings of cosmoses of other 'scales,' have their experiences of a definite duration for all their perceptions and manifestations; and, also, like them, they sense the flow of Time by the comparison of the duration of the phenomena around them.

> "Exactly like the beings of other cosmoses, they are born, they grow up, they unite and separate for what are called 'sex-results' and they also fall sick and suffer, and ultimately like everything existing in which Objective Reason has not become fixed, they are destroyed forever.

> "For the entire process of the existence of these infinitesimal beings

*of this smallest world, Time of a definite proportionate duration also ensues from all the surrounding phenomena which are manifested in the given 'cosmic-scale.'*

*"For them also, Time of definite length is required for the processes of their arising and formation as well as for various events in the process of their existence up to their complete final destruction.*

*"In the whole course of the process of existence of the beings of this drop of water also, corresponding sequential definite what are called 'passages' of the flow of Time are also required.*

*"A definite time is required for their joys and for their sorrows, and, in short, for every other kind of indispensable being-experiencing, down to what are called 'runs-of-bad- luck,' and even to 'periods-of-thirst-for-self-perfection.'*

*"I repeat, among them also, the process of the flow of Time has its harmonious sequence, and this sequence ensues from the totality of all the phenomena surrounding them.*

*"The duration of the process of the flow of Time is generally perceived and sensed in the same way by all the aforementioned cosmic Individuals and by the already completely formed what are called 'instinctivized' units but only with that difference which ensues from the difference in the presences and states, at the given moment, of these cosmic arisings.*[10]

When we start to apply this idea to beings at a much larger scale, the idea that a  Planet or Sun or Galaxy experiences its lifetime as merely 70-80 years, may seem strange. But, in truth, we know almost nothing about how such beings live their lives. We can only guess at their experiences.

## As Above, So Below

This brings us face to face with a fundamental question: "What can we know of life outside of the domain of Nature?"

The primary way of envisioning the life of cosmoses beyond our scale, whether much larger like a star or much smaller like a cell, is by

---

[10] *The Tales, Ch XLIII, Beelzebub's Opinion of War, p125-126*

analogy. The often-cited motto, originally expressed in the so-called *Emerald Tablet of Hermes Trismegistus*, is:

**As Above, So Below.**

This concept, of all cosmoses existing according to the same pattern is also one interpretation of the six-pointed Star of David, which is often to be encountered in occult literature. The image in *Figure 3*, shows such an illustration.

This idea is exploited frequently and skillfully by Gurdjieff in *The Tales*. There are two distinct aspects to this, which need to be explained, as Gurdjieff employs them both.

The first is more analogy that allegory, comparing two cosmoses of different scales. At times Gurdjieff does this in a sophisticated way switching,

*Figure 3. The Star of David*

as it were, from one cosmos to another. At first he seems to be discussing, say, the planetary world, but he abruptly switches to the psychological world – often without the reader noticing.

It is at once analogical and allegorical.

The second aspect is what can be called the "Psychological Drama." In psychological dramas, the events of the outer world represent events of the inner world of an individual. The characters in the drama are aspects of the psyche. Gurdjieff also employs this kind of allegory in all three series of his writings.

Excellent examples of psychological dramas are provided by Shakespeare.

## Shakespeare and the Psychological Dramas

One of the rarely discussed aspects of a significant number of Shakespeare's plays is the bard's use of allegory. Take for example, *The Tragedy of Othello, the Moor of Venice.*

The historical backdrop to the play is the Ottoman–Venetian War (1570–1573) where two armies are fighting over the Island of Cyprus, a possession of the Venetian Republic. Othello is a Moorish general who commands the Venetian army defending Cyprus.

He has recently married Desdemona, a beautiful and wealthy Venetian lady much younger than himself, against the wishes of her father. The other major character in the play is Iago, who is angry with Othello from the outset, because Othello overlooked him and instead promoted Cassio to the role of lieutenant. Thus Iago remained in the lesser rank of ensign.

In the course of the play, Iago cleverly and maliciously provokes his master's jealously leading him to believe that his wife, Desdemona, is being unfaithful to him. Ultimately he provokes Othello into killing the blameless Desdemona, and then Othello kills himself.

When we move from the literal story to the allegory, we see Iago as as aspect of false personality – a consequence of the properties of the organ Kundabuffer – the representative of the Devil himself within us. He leads Othello into temptation. The noble Othello can be viewed as the better side of personality that Iago manages to drag down. Desdemona can be viewed as essence, the passive side, who is ultimately destroyed by false personality.

The more you examine the play in this way, the more it becomes clear that it is a psychological drama, with all the characters depicting aspects of the inner world of a single person. The outcome is a tragedy.

Many other Shakespeare plays can be viewed in this way, including *King Lear, Hamlet, MacBeth, The Tempest,* and *Twelfth Night.*

## The Gospel Psychological Dramas

The gospels contain two important psychological dramas. The first is the Christmas story, the second the crucifixion.

The Christmas story is the story of the virgin birth of the body Kesdjan (or Astral Body). It is a virgin birth because the body Kesdjan is born entirely of one's own inner efforts. The birth is announced by a messenger (angel or perhaps the higher emotional center). It takes place in a lowly stable, away from the bustle of an Inn (personality). It is attended by shepherds and their flocks (the many 'I's) and by three kings (the moving center, the lower emotional and the lower intellectual center). King Herod (false personality) wishes to destroy all the newly born, but Mary, Joseph and the baby Jesus flee to Egypt (a higher realm).

The story of the crucifixion – the birth of the soul – is distinctly different. With the birth of the body Kesdjan, the higher parts of an individual accompany and witness the birth; they move towards the event, to become witnesses. In the crucifixion, Jesus is condemned by the authorities, and almost everyone involved with him seems to abandon him.

Following the Last Supper, Judas betrays Jesus with a kiss. This is the precursor to the arrest of Jesus by the Temple guards of the Sanhedrin in the Garden of Gethsemane. At the gate to the garden, Peter is accused of knowing Christ, and he denies knowledge of him three times.

The Sanhedrin, elders of the Judaic religion in Jerusalem, a tribunal that had the power to arrest and put on trial. Jesus is accused and found guilty of: violating the Sabbath law by healing on the Sabbath, threatening to destroy the Jewish Temple, practicing sorcery, exorcising people by the power of demons, and claiming to be the Messiah. Jesus responds to his accusers with silence – not mounting any defense.

Jesus is passed to Pontius Pilate the following morning. Pilate can find no fault with him, but when Pilate asks the crowd to choose between Jesus and Barabas, Jesus is condemned by the crowd.

Thus, Jesus is condemned to death. He is then made to carry his cross to the place of crucifixion. He falls three times as he makes his way to Golgotha. He is scourged, stripped of his garments and made to wear a crown of thorns.

He is nailed to the cross, and the letters INRI are attached to the cross above his head – mocking him. INRI stands for "Jesus of Nazareth, King of the Jews, in Latin. Among the few words that Jesus is heard to say while on the cross are:

*"My God, My God, why have you forsaken me?"*

Jesus is rejected and condemned by the representatives of his people (the Sanhedrin), is betrayed by Judas, Peter denies him thrice, he is condemned by the crowd, Pontius Pilate washes his hands, he is humiliated on the way to his place of execution and, before being nailed to the cross, he is stripped of his clothes and tortured.

He sacrifices everything and it seems that even God deserts him.

This is a dramatic rendition for the birth of the soul. All of the characters in this allegory can be viewed as elements of our inner world: The Sanhedrin, the disciples Judas and Peter, Pontius Pilate, Barabas, the crowd, the Roman soldiers who scourged him, crowned him with thorns, and gambled for his clothes, the two thieves crucified each side of him, and Mary Magdalene and Jesus himself are aspects of the inner world, in the birth of the soul.

## *The Tales* as Scripture

Gurdjieff's writings are the only examples of scripture created in the modern age and the only scripture that was published first in English for an English speaking audience. It is similar to other scripture in many ways; extensive use of metaphor, parables and allegory, its poetic nature, its rhythm when read out loud. It contains an explanation of the creation. Although explained in words that are difficult to digest, it includes an explanation of "objective science" and hence many of the mechanisms of life at the biological level and the planetary level and the cosmic level. Like The Gospels it is awash with psychological truth.

It is unlike any other important works of scripture: *The Torah, The Old and New Testaments, The Koran* or *The Tao Te Ching.* This is perhaps because, like those books, it was written for its time - and it was written by a true master of languages. For those who are willing to give themselves to the book, it is a gift, alive with practical knowledge.

Gurdjieff said:

> … *But I can explain now everything simply. For example, in the First Series, I know there is everything one must know. It is a very interesting book.*
>
> *Everything is there. All that exists, all that has existed, all that can exist. The beginning, the end, all the secrets of the creation of the world; all is there. But one must understand, and to understand depends on one's individuality. The more man has been instructed in a certain way, the more he can see.*
>
> *Subjectively, everyone is able to understand according to the level he occupies, for it is an objective book, and everyone should understand something in it. One person understands one part, another a thousand times more. Now, find a way to put your attention on understanding all of the First Series. This will be your task, and it is a good way to fix a real attention. If you can put real attention on the First Series, you can have a real attention in life.*[1]

He also said:

> *I have buried in this book certain bones, so that certain dogs with great curiosity and strong scent may dig down to them, and, strange thing, when they have done so, are men.*[2]

---

[1] *Paris meetings 1938, Meeting Fifteen*
[2] *Note Books of L. S. M.: ORAGE LECTURES [1927-1928] by Lawrence S Morris*

# GURDJIEFF AND KUNDABUFFER

# The Birth of the Moon

*"He who knows what his moon is and does can understand the cosmos."*
*~ Gurdjieff*

Chapter IX of *The Tales, The Cause of the Genesis of the Moon*, describes Beelzebub's observation of the birth of the Moon from the planet Mars with the following words:

> *"We were still fully absorbed in the bustle of organizing everything externally necessary for a more or less tolerable existence in the midst of that Nature absolutely foreign to us, when suddenly, on one of the very busiest days, the whole planet Mars was shaken, and a little later such an 'asphyxiating' stink arose that at first it seemed that everything in the Universe had been mixed up with something, one might say 'indescribable.'*

> *"Only after a considerable time had passed and when the said stink had gone, did we recover and gradually make out what had happened.*

> *"We understood that the cause of this terrible phenomenon was just that same planet Earth which from time to time approached very near to our planet Mars and which therefore we had possibilities of observing clearly, sometimes even without a 'Teskooano.'*

> *"For reasons we could not yet comprehend, this planet, it transpired, had 'burst' and two fragments detached from it had flown off into space.*

> *"I have already told you that this solar system was then still being*

*formed and was not yet 'blended' completely with what is called 'The-Harmony-of-Reciprocal-Maintenance-of-All-Cosmic-Concentrations.'*

*"It was subsequently learned that in accordance with this said 'General-Cosmic-Harmony-of-Reciprocal-Maintenance-of-All-Cosmic-Concentrations' there had also to function in this system a comet of what is called 'vast orbit' still existing and named the comet 'Kondoor.'*

*"And just this very comet, although it was then already concentrated, was actualizing its 'full path' for only the first time.*

*"As certain competent Sacred Individuals also later confidentially explained to us, the line of the path of the said comet had to cross the line on which the path of that planet Earth also lay; but as a result of the erroneous calculations of a certain Sacred Individual concerned with the matters of World-creation and World-maintenance, the time of the passing of each of these concentrations through the point of intersection of the lines of their paths coincided, and owing to this error the planet Earth and the comet 'Kondoor' collided, and collided so violently that from this shock, as I have already told you, two large fragments were broken off from the planet Earth and flew into space.*

*"This shock entailed these serious consequences because on account of the recent arising of this planet, the atmosphere which might have served as a buffer in such a case had not yet had time to be completely formed upon it.*[3]

The image of a comet colliding with a planet resembles the image of a sperm attaching to and fertilizing an ovum. The words "the whole planet Mars was shaken," are suggestive of an orgasm.

*… and a little later such an 'asphyxiating' stink arose that at first it seemed that everything in the Universe had been mixed up with something, one might say 'indescribable,'*[4]

The word 'asphyxiating,' wrapped in quotes by Gurdjieff has a surprising etymology, its meaning having changed over the years. It is as follows:

---

[3] *The Tales, Ch IX, The Cause of the Genesis of the Moon, p81-82*
[4] *The Tales, Ch IX, The Cause of the Genesis of the Moon, p81*

**asphyxia (n.)** 1706, "stoppage of pulse, absence of pulse," from Modern Latin *asphyxia* "stopping of the pulse," from Greek *asphyxia* "stopping of the pulse," from *a* "not" + *sphyzein* "to throb, to beat violently." The later and now dominant meaning of "suffocation, extreme condition caused by lack of oxygen in the blood" is from 1778. The word experienced a curious change of meaning.

**stink (v.)** This comes from the Old English *stincan* meaning "to emit a smell of any kind; to exhale; rise (of dust, vapor, etc.)" Old English had *swote stincan* "to smell sweet," but also to smell in the offensive sense. This negative meaning predominated by mid-13c. Stink is the root of stench. The word smell is now trending in the same way, towards meaning an offensive odor.

Using this etymology, the *asphyxiating stink* can be read as meaning "an odor consequent on the cessation of throbbing." Sexual intercourse involves both odorous secretions and the cessation of throbbing.

The statement, *it seemed that everything in the Universe had been mixed up with something, one might say 'indescribable'* is curious. Etymologically, "indescribable" means, as you would expect, "unable to be described, interpreted, explained" – but "everything in the Universe" is less certain. If this is an allegorical reference to the impregnation of a woman, then "everything in the Universe" may simply signify her whole body.

## Comets in *The Tales*

The comet *Kondoor* appears not to be a comet in the astronomical sense, as it is referred to as "*a comet of what is called 'vast orbit' still existing.*" Certainly comets can have vast orbits but when they collide with planets, as the comet Shoemaker-Levy 9 did with Jupiter, in July 1994, they are completely destroyed. And yet in *The Tales* the comet *Kondoor* is described as "*still existing.*" And incidentally, Shoemaker-Levy 9's impact with Jupiter did not bring about the birth of a moon.

The meaning of the name *Kondoor* is debatable. *Kon* is likely the Latin prefix *con*, meaning "with or together."

The meaning of the morpheme *door* is less certain. If it is the Armenian *dur* then, it may mean "door," "threshold," "entrance" or "beginning." This could indicate a sperm as a doorway to a new being.

Now consider, this excerpt from much later in the book.

> *into the forms of particular functions existing there under the names of, 'envy,' 'jealousy,' 'sandoor' (i.e., wishing the death or weakness of others), and so on.*[5]

Gurdjieff's inclusion of the word *sandoor* in this text is odd, as the term is mentioned nowhere else in *The Tales*. So it may be his way of providing help in discovering the meaning of the morpheme *door*. This morpheme occurs in only three of his constructed words and names: in *Kondoor, Sandoor* and *Moordoorten*.

So one possibility is that the morpheme *door* relates to vital energy. Clearly sperm carry vital energy, so *Kondoor* would imply "with vital energy." *Sandoor* might possibly be *sans* (Latin for "without") meaning without vital energy.

*Moordoorten* (masturbation) might equate to the "waste of vital energy." In Armenian, "mur" means "mind, brain or intellect," and *ten* is the Turkish suffix meaning "from" – implying "an intellectual practice that wastes energy."

In general, in *The Tales,* comets seem to signify sexual energy or influence.

## Sakoor

If we consider other comets, the solar system Beelzebub calls Vuanik is home to a comet named Sakoor or 'Madcap.' It is because of that comet that the ship Karnak is obliged to "delay its falling," which in turn prompts Beelzebub to begin recounting tales of his experiences to Hassein. The captain of the Karnak advises:

> *"… if we follow our intended course, then our ship, after two 'Kil-*

---

[5] *The Tales, Ch XXXVIII. Religion, p718*

*prenos,' will pass through the solar system 'Vuanik.'*

"*But just through where our ship must pass, there must also pass, about a 'Kilpreno' before, the great comet belonging to that solar system and named 'Sakoor' or, as it is sometimes called, the 'Madcap.'*

"*So if we keep to our proposed course, we must inevitably traverse the space through which this comet will have to pass.*[6]

In a footnote we read:

*The word "Kilpreno" in the language of Beelzebub means a certain period of time, equal approximately to the duration of the flow of time which we call an "hour."*[7]

Curiously, *Kil* indicates "the space between the tips of the thumb and forefinger" in Armenian, and in Turkish it means "a hair's breadth," The morpheme *preno* is less certain. It may be a distortion of the French *prendre* (to take) or possibly it derives from the Slovenian or Croatian languages, where *prenos* means "transfer." If so, then Kilpreno indicates an hour, which is seen as the passage of a very short amount of time. This aligns with the idea that time passes 389 time more slowly for beings from Karatas. Thus an hour of our human time would equate to just under ten seconds of Beelzebub's and Hassein's experience of time.

The etymology of Vuanik seems to be a combination of French and Slavic languages. *Nik* is the same as the suffix *er* in English (as in baker or cobbler). In French *Vu* is "seen," *a* is has. So Vuanik suggests "one who has seen."

"Madcap" means literally "mad head," implying hot-headed or even crazy.

The name *Sakoor*, can be split into *Sak* and *koor*. *Sak* means "sack" or "bag" or "container" in many languages. *Koor* means "blind" in both Armenian and Persian – implying, perhaps, that the comet *Sakoor* brings blindness to one who has seen.

---

[6] *The Tales, Ch III. The Cause of the Delay in the Falling of the Ship Karnak, p56*
[7] *The Tales, Ch III. The Cause of the Delay in the Falling of the Ship Karnak, p56*

Elsewhere in *The Tales*, when describing the operation of the ships constructed with the system of St Venoma, Beelzebub comments:

*"It was particularly difficult to steer them in those spheres where there was a great aggregation of 'comets.'*[8]

In our view, the spaceships of *The Tales* are a means for moving from one state to another. Personal acts of self-remembering, non-identification and non-considering, for example, are means of doing this – moving for example from normal mechanical behavior to greater awareness. In *The Tales,* when Gurdjieff uses the term "sphere" he is speaking of an area of influence, such as for example the atmosphere of another person.

"The implication might then be that it is difficult to maintain your state when in the presence of someone who is alive with sexual energy. In respect of Vuanik and its comet Sakoor, we read:

*"Your Right Reverence of course knows that this 'Madcap' comet always leaves in its track a great deal of 'Zilnotrago\* which on entering the planetary body of a being disorganizes most of its functions until all the 'Zilnotrago' is volatilized out of it.*[9]

## Zilnotrago

A footnote at the bottom of page 56 explains the word *Zilnotrago* as follows:

*The word "Zilnotrago" is the name of a special gas similar to what we call "cyanic acid."*[10]

Etymologically *Zilno* (or *silno*) means "strongly" in several Slavic languages including Russian (*zil'no*). Its etymology is uncertain. However in Slovenian *zilno* can mean "vascular," i.e., relating to the blood system and vessels and in Slovak, it means "venous." We suspect it is more likely that Gurdjieff intends the meaning "strongly."

*Tragos* means a "billy goat" in Greek, also "the goat-like smell of armpits" and "the age of puberty." Thus we can think of it as a sub-

---

[8] *The Tales, Ch IV. The Law of Falling, p69*

[9] *The Tales, Ch III. The Cause of the Delay in the Falling of the Ship Karnak, p56*

[10] *The Tales, Ch III. The Cause of the Delay in the Falling of the Ship Karnak, p56*

stance relating to sex – perhaps relating to the **asphyxiating stink** mentioned on page 81. So Zilnotrago seems to mean "a strong goat-like odor."

Note that the English word "tragedy" comes from the Greek *tragos*, goat and *oide*, which means song. Thus tragedy originally meant "goat song." It is presumed, but not known for sure, that tragedy refers to a song that a Greek chorus would sing prior to the ritual sacrifice of a goat.

If we take the alternative possible meaning for *Zilnotrago*, as blood of a goat, then it may refer to the sacrifice of two-brained beings, which we take to mean, allegorically, the suppression of the emotions. Perhaps even both meanings are intended.

The mention of *cyanic acid* is surprising. The chemical formula for cyanic acid is HCNO. It is thus a combination of one atom each of Hydrogen, Carbon, Nitrogen and Oxygen. In *In Search of the Miraculous* Gurdjieff refers to substances as Hydrogens, Carbons as substances through which the active force is manifesting, Oxygens as substances through which the passive force is manifesting and Nitrogens as substances though which the neutralizing force is manifesting. This may simply be a coincidence or a direct reference to that from Gurdjieff (but if so, why?).

Note that the text says *similar to what we call "cyanic acid."* The same chemical formula (HCNO) also applies to other substances including isocyanic acid and fulminic acid (they have the same four atoms but the molecular bonding is different). They are "similar" in that way to cyanic acid, but if he was referring to either he would probably say so.

Such substances when immersed in water break up into ammonia and carbon dioxide which are common excrescences of men and animals.

They generally *volitalize* quickly. (The word "volatile" comes from the Latin verb *volare*, "to fly.")

Cyanic acid is of course a poison, and fulminic acid is used to make detonators for explosives. So, if nothing else, Gurdjieff is implying that the influence of *zilnotrago* is to be avoided. And as the text explains the Karnak avoided the *zilnotrago*:

> *"I thought at first," continued the captain, "of avoiding the 'Zilnotrago' by steering the ship around these spheres, but for this a long detour would be necessary which would greatly lengthen the time of our passage. On the other hand, to wait somewhere until the 'Zilnotrago' is dispersed would take still longer.*[11]

The action the Karnak actually took was to go no further until the *zilnotrago* had dispersed. So the question is: "what is Gurdjieff trying to tell us here, allegorically."

One possible answer is that certain interactions with others are to be avoided. In this instance we suspect that exposing oneself to *zilnotrago* equates to responding positively to flirtatious behavior. In The Work, when certain unnecessary and unhelpful interactions appear to commence, the normal recourse is silence (the Karnak stays where it is) or to walk away (the Karnak takes a detour).

Note that there is no evidence of flirtatious behavior by Beelzebub throughout *The Tales*. Beelzebub does not even select his wife, as the text makes plain...

> *"On the planet Mars I was indeed expected by several beings of our tribe who had newly arrived from the planet Karatas. Among them, by the way, was also your grandmother who, according to the indications of the chief Zirlikners of the planet Karatas, had been assigned to me as the passive half for the continuance of my line."*[12]

Beelzebub does not engage in any kind of courting to select his wife, he is simply assigned an appropriate female by a Zirlikner (doctor) of his tribe. Elsewhere in *The Tales* it is said that such doctors use astrologer, to determine appropriate matches.

---

[11] *The Tales, Ch III. The Cause of the Delay in the Falling of the Ship Karnak, p56-57*
[12] *The Tales, Ch XX. The Third Flight of Beelzebub to the Planet Earth, p206*

We encounter comets in a solar system much later in *The Tales* in the system called *Salzmanino*, which proves necessary for the Karnak to avoid. The text is as follows:

> *"I do not know just what obstacles there were then for the captain of the ship Omnipresent, but in the present case, on the direct route between the holy planet Purgatory and the planet Deskaldino, there lies the solar system called Salzmanino, in which there are many of those cosmic concentrations which, for purposes of the general cosmic Trogoautoegocratic process, are predetermined for the transformation and radiation of the substances Zilnotrago; and therefore the direct falling of our ship Karnak, unhindered, through this system, will scarcely be possible.*[13]

## Salzmanino

In the *Salzmanino* system there are many cosmic concentrations which, for purposes of the general cosmic Trogoautoegocratic process, are predetermined for the transformation and radiation of the substances *Zilnotrago*.

This is a different situation from the system *Vuanik*. The problem is not *Zilnotrago* from the passage of a single comet, where one can simply wait it out. Instead the whole system of *Salzmanino* is to be avoided completely because of the cosmic concentrations in it that radiate *Zilnotrago* and do so naturally, part of the Trogoautoegocratic process.

It is possible although perhaps unlikely that Gurdjieff, with the name *Salzmanino*, is referring to Madame de Salzmann, Alexander de Salzmann, Michel de Salzmann or any others of that line. The surname Salzmann has a double 'n' whereas *Salzmanino* does not.

A possible etymology here is as follows: *Salz* is German for "salt," *man* is English for man, and *ino* is a common Italian suffix denoting "little," as for example in "buffalino," meaning "little clown." Putting this together we can take *Salzmanino* to mean "man of little salt."

---

[13] *The Tales, Ch XXX. The Change in the Appointed Course of the Falling of the Transspace Ship Karnak, p659*

"Salt" is a well known New Testament symbol. Jesus says to his disciples:

> *"Ye are the salt of the earth: but if the salt have lost its savour, wherewith shall it be salted?" (Matthew 5.13).*

It can be taken to symbolize the accumulation of understanding or alternatively, the growth of essence in the gradual crystallization of a body Kesdjan. In which case "man of little salt" would indicate normal man, whose activity naturally involves aggregations of comets.

## Moon and Anulios

The description of the two fragments which broke away from the planet Earth following its collision with the comet, is as follows:

> *"of these two fragments, the larger was named 'Loonderperzo' and the smaller 'Anulios'; and the ordinary three-brained beings who afterwards arose and were formed on this planet also at first called them by these names; but the beings of later times called them differently at different periods, and in most recent times the larger fragment has come to be called Moon, but the name of the smaller has been gradually forgotten.*

*Loonderperzo* possibly requires more effort to unravel. *Loon* can be taken as the French *lune* meaning "moon," *der*, German for "that or which" and *perzo* could be French slang for "lost." So possibly "lost Moon." Alternatively in Dutch, Loon means "wage," and *Loonder* means a "wager or bet," so possibly "lost wager." Neither seems to fit well. It would be more appropriate if it meant "something for which payment is made." We are unsure of the meaning.

Anulios is clearer. This is most likely a combination of Anu and ilios ($\eta\lambda\iota o\zeta$), the Greek word for Sun, from which we get Helios, the ancient Greek god of the Sun. *Samlios*, the capital of Atlantis (*p110*) is a similar word, composed of *Sam* a Russian and Slavic word for "self" and *lios* which we can take to be the Sun or an equivalent cosmic concentration. Thus the capital city *Samlios* to be the place of self. If we take Atlantis as representing childhood then Samlios can be thought of as the center of 'essence.'

## *About Anu*

*Anu* is the supreme deity and ancestor of all other deities in the ancient Sumerian religion. According to Wikipedia, he is described in one Mesopotamian text as the one "who contains the entire universe." He dwelt in the highest heavenly regions, and it was believed that the stars were his soldiers.

He is mentioned in the verse below from The Epic of Gilgamesh which Gurdjieff quotes in *Meetings With Remarkable Men*, noting that the text of the poem, translated from cuneiform tablets, was identical to the version known to his father, which had been passed down to Ashokhs over thousands of years.

> *I will tell thee, Gilgamesh,*
> *Of a mournful mystery of the Gods:*
> *How once, having met together,*
> *They resolved to flood the land of Shuruppak.*
> *Clear-eyed Ea, saying nothing to his father, Anu,*
> *Nor to the Lord, the great Enlil,*
> *Nor to the spreader of happiness, Nemuru,*
> *Nor even the underworld prince, Enua,*
> *Called to him his son Ubara-Tut;*
> *Said to him: "Build thyself a ship,*
> *Take with thee thy near ones,*
> *And what birds and beasts thou wilt;*
> *Irrevocably have the Gods resolved*
> *To flood the land of Shuruppak."*[14]

Bearing in mind that Anu is the dominant god of the Summarians, we take *Anulios* to indicate the higher centers in Man, both of them. So the impact of the comet *Kondor* caused a lower, fairly large fragment, the Moon, to break away from Earth and a smaller less visible fragment, the higher centers, also to split off.

In respect of the awareness of this smaller fragment we read:

> *"It is interesting to notice here that the beings of a continent on that*

---

[14] *Meetings With Remarkable Men, p35*

*planet called 'Atlantis,' which afterwards perished, still knew of this second fragment of their planet and also called it 'Anulios,' but the beings of the last period of the same continent, in whom the results of the consequences of the properties of that organ called 'Kundabuffer' – about which, it now seems, I shall have to explain to you even in great detail – had begun to be crystallized and to become part of their common presences, called it also 'Kimespai,' the meaning of which for them was 'Never-Allowing-One-to-Sleep-in-Peace.'*[15]

We read about Atlantis later in *The Tales*, where it also notes that the consequences of the properties of the organ Kundabuffer were beginning to influence the behavior of some of the population. At that time they referred to this fragment as *Kimespai*.

The meaning 'Never-Allowing-One-to-Sleep-in-Peace' makes sense if we think of the higher emotional center as the seat of conscience. If one behaves from the crystallized consequences of the properties of Kundabuffer, at times conscience is likely to manifest and may prevent one from sleeping in peace.

The etymology of Kimespai may possibly be as follows: *Ki* was the earth goddess in the Sumerian Religion and the chief consort of Anu. *Mespai* could possibly be the French *m'espai* which has the sense of "I am sparse" implying "I rarely manifest." This suggests the higher emotional center.

*"Contemporary three-brained beings of this peculiar planet do not know of this former fragment of their planet, chiefly because its comparatively small size and the remoteness of the place of its movement make it quite invisible to their sight, and also because no 'grandmother' ever told them that once upon a time any such little satellite of their planet was known.*

*"And if any of them should by chance see it through their good, but nevertheless child's toy of theirs called telescope, he would pay no attention to it, mistaking it simply for a big aerolite.*[16]

---

[15] *The Tales, Ch IX, The Cause of the Genesis of the Moon, p85*
[16] *The Tales, Ch IX, The Cause of the Genesis of the Moon, p85*

Gurdjieff uses "grandmother" as a symbol of wisdom and knowledge passed down by word of mouth – a tradition that is less common than it used to be.

Technically (geologically) an aerolite is similar to a meteorite but distinctive in that it consists of silicate minerals rather than metallic ones. However there is also an etymological difference. *Aerolite* consists of *aero* meaning "of the air," and *lite* is a suffix used to indicate something of a mineral nature. Meteorite is similar, with meteor meaning "of the atmosphere" rather than "of the air."

The specific meaning, for meteorite as "fireball in the sky, or shooting star" is from 1590s. Prior to that atmospheric phenomena were formerly classified as aerial meteors (born of the wind), aqueous meteors (rain, snow, hail), luminous meteors (aurora, rainbows), and igneous meteors (lightning, shooting stars). A meteoroid is the name given to the object while it is in space. It becomes a meteorite only when it enters the atmosphere.

The assertion is that if we observed *Anulios* through a telescope we would assume it was an aerolite (i.e. something not in orbit around the Earth).

# Gurdjieff and Kundabuffer

# CHAPTER V

# Laws of The Solar System

*"Nature takes her orders from above and she carries them out."*
*~ Gurdjieff*

B eelzebub informs us that the news of the collision between the comet *Kondoor* and Earth, described in the text as a general cosmic misfortune, was immediately reported to our *ENDLESSNESS*.

*"In consequence of this report, a whole commission consisting of Angels and Archangels, specialists in the work of World-creation and World-maintenance, under the direction of the Most Great Archangel Sakaki, was immediately sent from the Most Holy Sun Absolute to that solar system 'Ors.'*

*"The Most High Commission came to our planet Mars since it was the nearest to the planet Earth and from this planet of ours began its investigations.*

*"The sacred members of this Most High Commission at once quieted us by saying that the apprehended danger of a catastrophe on a great cosmic scale had already passed.*

*"And the Arch-Engineer Archangel Algamatant was good enough to explain to us personally that in all probability what had happened was as follows:*

*"'The broken-off fragments of the planet Earth had lost the momentum they received from the shock before they had reached the limit of that part of space which is the sphere of this planet, and*

*hence, according to the "Law of Falling," these fragments had be-
gun to fall back towards their fundamental piece.*

*"'But they could no longer fall upon their fundamental piece, be-
cause in the meantime they had come under the cosmic law called
"Law-of-Catching-Up" and were entirely subject to its influence,
and they would therefore now make regular elliptic orbits around
their fundamental piece, just as the fundamental piece, namely, the
planet Earth, made and makes its orbit around its sun "Ors."*[17]

The immediate assessment of the high commission was that the
danger of a catastrophe on a great cosmic scale had passed. Arch-Engineer Archangel Algamatant explained that the broken off fragments had not escaped the planet Earth, but instead they now
occupied an orbit around it.

Algamatant talks in terms of the limit of *that part of space which is
the sphere of this planet*. Naturally, from the way it is worded, we can
think in terms of the two fragments, Moon and Anulios acquiring
momentum from the impact but failing to escape the gravitational
pull of the Earth and hence both settling into an orbit.

However, if that is the intended meaning then Algamatant has described it in a very strange manner. If we were using the terminology
of physics we would not say *that part of space which is the sphere of this
planet* and no doubt we would use the word gravity, which Algamatant does not mention at all, despite his title, Arch-Engineer. Instead Algamatant mentions both the *Law of Falling* and the *Law-of-
Catching-Up*.

## The Law of Falling

In Chapter IV of *The Tales*, St. Venoma's formulation of the *Law of
Falling* is as follows:

*"'Everything existing in the World falls to the bottom. And the
bottom for any part of the Universe is its nearest "stability," and this
said "stability" is the place or the point upon which all the lines of
force arriving from all directions converge.*

---

[17] *The Tales, Ch IX, The Cause of the Genesis of the Moon, p82-83*

*"The centers of all the suns and of all the planets of our Universe are just such points of "stability." They are the lowest points of those regions of space upon which forces from all directions of the given part of the Universe definitely tend and where they are concentrated. In these points there is also concentrated the equilibrium which enables suns and planets to maintain their position.'*

*"In this formulation of his, Saint Venoma said further that everything when dropped into space, wherever it may be, tends to fall on one or another sun or on one or another planet, according to which sun or planet the given part of space belongs to, where the object is dropped, each sun or planet being for the given sphere the 'stability' or bottom.*[18]

It is quite clear from this description that *The Law of Falling* is not the same as the Law of Gravity. Gurdjieff's text may fool the casual reader into assuming there's some equivalence, but the words tell a an entirely different story.

The defining difference between these two laws is the concept of a *bottom* or *stability*. The Law of Gravity does not any such idea.

In general a *stability* is a characteristic of a system or a person.

The etymology is as follows:

**stability** (n.) mid-14c., in respect of persons, "firmness of resolve, mental equilibrium" from Old French *stablete*, "firmness, solidity, stability; durability, constancy" from Latin *stabilitatem* "a standing fast, firmness," figuratively "security, steadfastness," from *stabilis* "steadfast, firm."

Most likely, *The Law of Falling* is one representation of the action of the Ray of Creation. The Ray of Creation is an octave that spans two aspects of the Absolute: the "Father Creator" as its highest level of vibration and the "Holy Firm" as its lowest level of vibration.

*Figure 4* provides a representation of this, as though from the side. The immediate level below the Absolute is the Sun Absolute (or All Worlds) in which the Absolute manifests as three rather than one.

---

[18] *The Tales, Ch IV, The Law of Falling, p66-67*

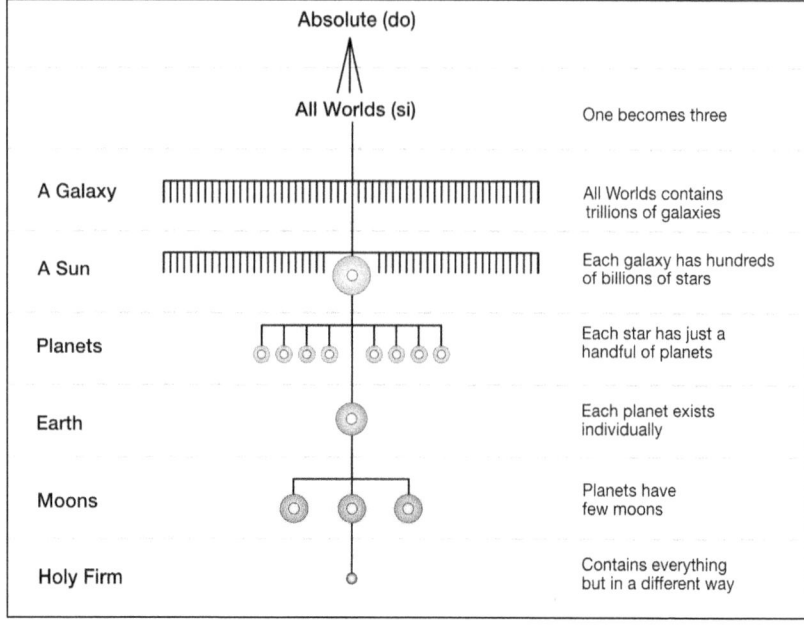

*Figure 4. The Ray of Creation, "from the side"*

Below that is the manifestation of the galaxies which modern science currently counts in the trillions. Within each galaxy, there exists a vast number of stars, which modern science currently estimates to be in the hundreds of billions.

The purpose of this diagram is to indicate the points of stability. They are:

> ... the lowest points of those regions of space upon which forces from all directions of the given part of the Universe definitely tend and where they are concentrated.[19]

As indicated in *Figure 4* and as the previous text stated, they are found at the centers of moons, planets and suns. All these heavenly bodies have, at their center, a lower *do*. That *do*, a manifestation of the Holy Firm, is the lower *do* for one specific Ray of Creation.

---

[19] *The Tales, Ch IV, The Law of Falling, p66*

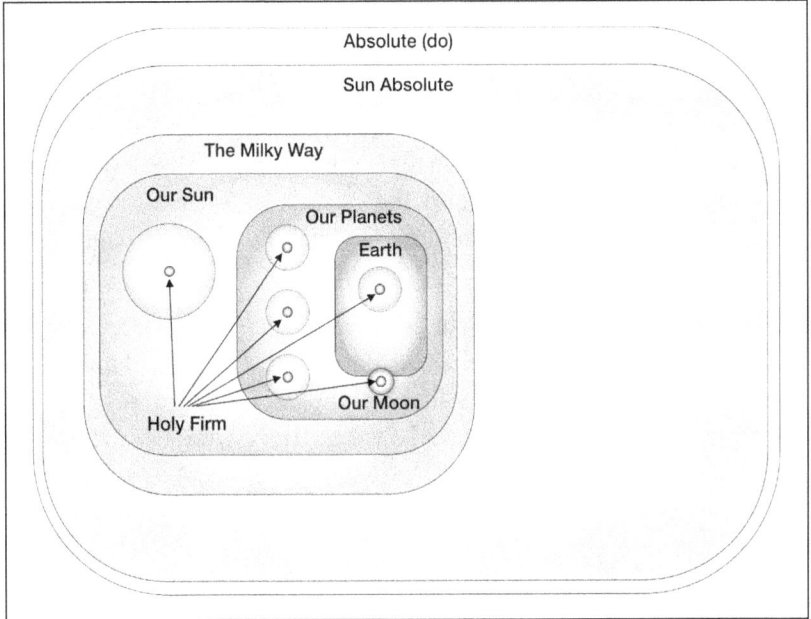

*Figure 5. The Ray of Creation, "from below"*

*Figure 4* is, a representation of an idea rather than a depiction of reality. *Figure 5* provides a different representation of one specific Ray of Creation as if from below. What is included here that was not included in *Figure 4* is the atmospheres of each heavenly body.

The Milky Way has an atmosphere, referred to as the ISM (Inter-Stellar Medium) that is known to extend tens of thousands of light years beyond any of the stars in The Milky Way. We can thus regard this atmosphere as the sphere of influence of The Milky Way. Everything dropped into space within this sphere will move towards (fall towards) the sun it is closest to in The Milky Way.

We can think of the boundary of The Milky Way shown in *Figure 5* as the Milky Way's ISM – the *part of space* which belongs to the galaxy. Similarly, in the diagram, the area labeled "Our Sun" is the atmosphere of our Sun and its boundary is the heliopause. If something were to be dropped anywhere within that boundary – that *part of space* – it would begin "to fall" towards the Sun.

The heliopause is the boundary of the region of space dominated by the Sun's magnetic field and solar wind – its atmosphere. Current estimates indicate that the heliopause is located about 123 astronomical units (AU) – about 11.4 billion miles – from the Sun, well beyond the orbit of Pluto and other outer planets. The distance between our sun's heliopause and the nearest heliopause of another star is estimated to be in the region of 62 trillion miles – roughly one light year.

The next *part of space* into which something could be dropped is in the atmosphere (magnetosphere) of one of the planets. Among the planets of our solar system, Jupiter has the largest magnetosphere. It is estimated 4.3 million miles in diameter. The Earth's is a maximum of 120,000 miles in diameter.

The Moon does not have an atmosphere as such. The Work insists that it is gradually acquiring one. As suggested in *Figure 5*, the Moon can be thought of partially living within the atmosphere (magnetosphere) of the Earth. It enters the magnetosphere of the Earth a few days before the full moon, remaining there for about five days before leaving.

## Holy The Firm

We can now consider Holy The Firm – the lower manifestation of The Absolute. Gurdjieff states that the *points of stability* are *the lowest points of those regions of space upon which forces from all directions of the given part of the Universe definitely tend and where they are concentrated.*[20]

We'll first consider the specific Ray of Creation that ends at the *point of stability* within our Sun. According to Gurdjieff, our sun was once a moon which evolved to become a planet and eventually evolved to become a sun. If it took such a path then within its core, aside from Holy The Firm, most likely it includes a moon and a planet and its Ray of Creation passes through those levels. It has both external planets and moons and an internal planet and moon.

---

[20] *The Tales, Ch IV, The Law of Falling, p66*

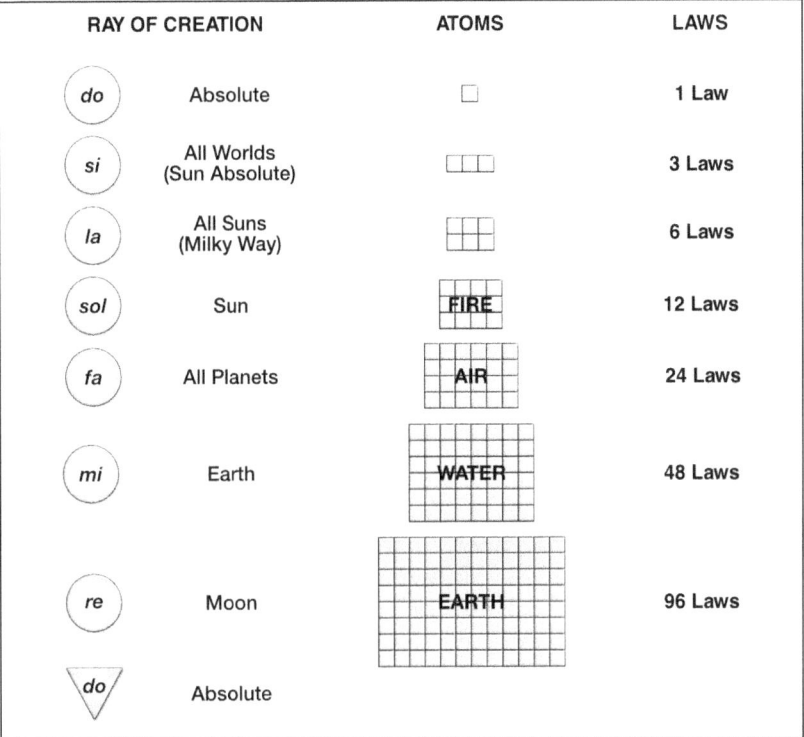

*Figure 6. The Ray, its Atoms and Laws*

Similarly if we consider the Ray of Creation which passes to the heart of any given planet, it too has an inner moon that corresponds in some way to its external moon (or moons).

## Litsvrtsi

In *The Tales*, Beelzebub refers to a second grade law called "Litsvrt-si"[21] that brings about "the aggregation of the homogenous." Such an aggregation is fundamental to the structure of the megalocosmos. *Figure 6* shows the Ray of Creation and the atoms that correspond to each of its levels.

According to The Work, the Universe is composed of these seven distinct types of matter.[22] The moon's matter is denser that the

---

[21] *The Tales, Ch XXXIX, The Holy Planet Purgatory, p758*
[22] *In Search of the Miraculous by Peter Ouspensky, p 87*

Earth's matter, which in turn is denser than matter of the planets and so on. Some types of matter are so rare and fine that from the perspective of modern science they are only hypothetical, and others are so fine that, as we are, we cannot recognized any of their characteristics at all.

As indicated in *Figure 6* on the previous page, the Ancient Greek classification of matter into Earth, Water, Air and Fire can be applied to the lower four of these seven levels.

- Matter corresponding to the Moon is called Earth
- Matter corresponding to the Earth is called Water
- Matter corresponding to the Planets is called Air
- Matter corresponding to the Sun is called Fire

Nevertheless, in examining our world we observe that all the different types of matter in the Universe are mixed together and can interpenetrate each other. The finer types of matter can permeate coarser ones, much like water saturates wood or gas penetrates water.

Litsvrtsi, the aggregation of the homogenous, leads to a predominance of particular atoms (of objective science) at particular levels. The actual Moon, even though it comprises atoms of all levels, has a predominance of the atoms of Moon that aggregate there. Similarly, due to Litsvrtsi, there is a predominance of atoms of Earth on Earth, atoms of Planets in the sphere of the planets and atoms of Sun in the heliosphere.

If we ignore all other planets and suns, and simply focus on the Earth, we notice that it also comprises atoms from these seven levels, which arrange themselves in seven layers corresponding to the Ray of Creation. Contemporary science lists many more layers including: the asthenosphere, lithosphere, pedosphere, hydrosphere, biosphere, anthroposphere, ionosphere and magnetosphere.[23] The existence of such layers implies the action of Litsvrtsi, with birds of a feather flocking together.

---

[23] *Gurdjieff's Hydrogens: The Ray Of Creation by R Bloor, p333*

The following equivalence suggests itself (starting at the lowest point):

- Holy The Firm: the core of the Earth
- Moon: the asthenosphere and lithosphere
- Earth: the pedosphere and hydrosphere
- Planets: the biosphere and anthroposphere
- Sun: the ionosphere and magnetosphere.

It is unlikely that such a layering can be brought about entirely by Litsvrtsi. Another force is in play, the force which science calls gravity. Not only do like elements and indeed life forms aggregate together, but the heavier ones sink to the lower levels and the lighter ones are raised to the higher levels.

## Gravity

Although conventional science has its preferred theories, gravity is currently a yet-to-be-explained phenomenon. Modern science prefers the Einsteinian theory, which dethroned the Newtonian theory a hundred years ago. And there are a variety of detractors – The Work being one such detractor. The phenomenon itself is not in dispute – measured and demonstrated long ago by Galileo.

A distinction between Newton's (and later Einstein's) formulation and that of Gurdjieff is the statement in *The Tales*:

> *In these points there is also concentrated the equilibrium which enables suns and planets to maintain their position.*[24]

Gurdjieff asserts that it is Holy The Firm that maintains the equilibrium of suns and planets, as opposed to science which insists it is the force of gravity.

Newton's formula for gravitational attraction has proved sufficient (without the need to involve any adjustment based on Einstein's gravitational ideas) to successfully launch thousands of satellites and space-shots, most of which have used the gravitational attraction of

---

[24] *The Tales, Ch IV, The Law of Falling, p66*

planets close to their route to navigate their way through the solar system.

It could thus be reasonably suggested that under the force of gravity those space-shots were in one way or another "falling" towards planets in the same way that the spaceships in *The Tales* fall towards planets or solar systems.

However, it is worth noting that there are many gravitational anomalies that have yet to be explained using the standard theory of gravity. Here is a list taken from a scientific website:[25]

1) Possible anomalous advances of planetary perihelia.
2) Unexplained orbital residuals of a recently discovered moon of Uranus (Mab).
3) The lingering unexplained secular increase of the eccentricity of the orbit of the Moon.
4) The so-called Faint Young Sun Paradox.
5) The secular decrease of the mass parameter of the Sun.
6) The Flyby Anomaly.
7) The Pioneer Anomaly.
8) The anomalous secular increase of the astronomical unit.

Above and beyond this set of gravitational curiosities, we have the fact that the so-called "n-body problem" (how to predict the individual motions of a group of *n* celestial objects interacting with each other gravitationally) is mathematically unsolved.

If that were not so then we would be able to explain exactly why the planets and moons carve out the orbits that they do – the idea being that if we know the weight of the planets we will be able to calculate their orbits because in precisely those and only those orbits the centrifugal force of the planetary orbit balances the centripetal force of the gravitational attraction between planet and sun.

Unfortunately we do not know the weight of the planets. The Earth is the only planet for which we can estimate the weight. We can cal-

---

[25] *https://www.worldscientific.com/doi/abs/10.1142/*

culate its gravitation constant from the motion of falling objects close to its surface - and that's it. Some scientists estimate the weight of the Sun using gravity and the Earth's orbit and then extent that calculation to estimate the orbit of other planets like Jupiter and Neptune.

But the mathematics of this doesn't work because the "n-body problem" remains unsolved, and anyway the planets seem to line up in a way that bears no relationship to gravitational force. And incidentally, the assumption being made is that there is no electromagnetic force involved at all, and yet most of the planets have magnetospheres and the heliosphere is awash with ionic plasma.

In respect of the points of stability having concentrated in them *the equilibrium which enables suns and planets to maintain their position*, it may make sense to cast gravity to the side and consider Blagg's Law and Bode's Law.

## *Bode's and Blagg's Laws*

Bode's Law (sometimes called Titius-Bode's Law) comprises a simple mathematical formula which predicts the distance between planets in a solar system. It suggests that, extending outward from the Sun, each planet should be about twice as far from the sun as the one before. Bode's law is not based upon any presumed astronomical force, simply a mathematical formula that provides an approximate fit to the orbits of the planets in our solar system.

The law can also be applied to calculate/predict the distances of the orbits of moons around their parent planet accurately. It has been applied with success to all the large planets in our solar system which have families of moons.

From the perspective of The Work, the idea that there is a natural placement for all the planets (and moons) makes sense. It would imply that (in some way) the planets seek to maintain a natural equilibrium. So the idea that in every planet a natural equilibrium is "concentrated in their point of stability," seems possible, even if we do not entirely understand how that happens.

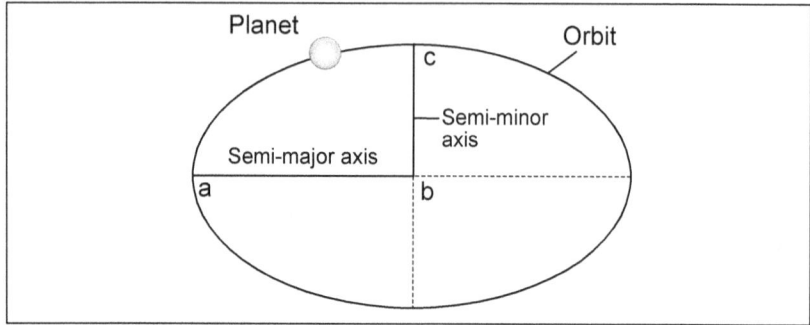

*Figure 7. Planetary Orbit*

With Bode's Law, it is important to note that the mathematical formula applies to the semi-major axis of a planet's (or moon's) elliptical orbit rather than its average orbital radius. This is the length *ab* shown in *Figure 7* above.

The elliptical orbits of the planets vary in respect of their shape, some being more "eccentric" than others. Bode's Law predicts that for each planet the semi-major axis will be:

$$a_n = 0.4 + 0.3 \times 2^n$$

Where the result is a number of astronomical units (one AU is the average distance from the Earth to the Sun). The first term (the constant 0.4) is the semi-major axis of Mercury. Then $a_0$ gives Venus, $a_1$ gives Earth and so on. This provides us with the results shown in *Table 1* on the next page.

The right hand side of this table shows the significantly more accurate results you can achieve by applying Blagg's Law rather than Bode's Law. In 1913 Mary Blagg improved on Bode's law by employing a geometric progress of 1.7275 (rather than 2, as in Bode's Law) and adding a periodic function. This is considerably more accurate. In Blagg's Law predicts Neptune fairly accurately, whereas Bode's Law does not.

It is also worth noting that its least accurate predictions are for the asteroid belt (which is composed of many fragmented asteroids with varying orbits) and Pluto, which has the most eccentric orbit of

| Orbits | | Bode's Law | | Blagg's Law | |
|---|---|---|---|---|---|
| Planet | Actual | Bode | Error | Blagg | Error |
| Mercury | 0.387 | 0.400 | 3.36% | 0.387 | 0.00% |
| Venus | 0.723 | 0.700 | 3.18% | 0.723 | 0.00% |
| Earth | 1.000 | 1.000 | 0.00% | 1.000 | 0.00% |
| Mars | 1.524 | 1.600 | 4.99% | 1.524 | 0.00% |
| Ceres | 2.769 | 2.800 | 1.12% | 2.67 | 3.58% |
| Jupiter | 5.204 | 5.200 | 0.08% | 5.200 | 0.08% |
| Saturn | 9.583 | 10.00 | 4.35% | 9.550 | 0.34% |
| Uranus | 19.22 | 19.60 | 1.98% | 19.23 | 0.05% |
| Neptune | 30.07 | 38.80 | 29.03% | 30.13 | 0.20% |
| Pluto | 39.48 | 77.20 | 95.54% | 41.8 | 5.88% |

*Table 1. Bode's Law and Blagg's Law*

any of the planets. Blagg's Law has more to recommend it than just that. It also produces surprisingly accurate results when used to predict the orbits of the moons of Jupiter, Saturn and Uranus. The results for the moons of Jupiter and Saturn are shown in *Table 2* (on the next page). The empty rows in the table indicate orbits where a moon would be expected to be, but where currently no moon exists. These can be thought of as empty slots which may be filled by moons in the future.

In the table, the moons whose names are given in parentheses are those that were discovered after Blagg's Law was formulated, and thus their discovery has validated the law. As the table shows there are no moons that do not correspond to some degree to a Blagg prediction. The moons like Himalia, Elara and Lysithea, which share the same Blagg value, have very similar orbits (in respect of the semi-major axis). Notice that these moons are the ones where Blagg's Law is least accurate. It is possible that such moons have not yet achieved a common harmony.

| Jupiter's Moons | | | Saturn's Moons | | |
|---|---|---|---|---|---|
| Moon | Orbit | Blagg | Moon | Orbit | Blagg |
| Amalthea | 0.429 | 0.429 | (Janus) | (0.538) | 0.54 |
| | | 0.708 | Mimas | 0.630 | 0.629 |
| Io | 1.000 | 1.000 | Enceladus | 0.808 | 0.807 |
| Europa | 1.592 | 1.592 | Tethys | 1.000 | 1.000 |
| Ganymede | 2.539 | 2.541 | Dione | 1.281 | 1.279 |
| Callisto | 4.467 | 4.467 | Rhea | 1.789 | 1.786 |
| | | 9.26 | | | 2.97 |
| | | 15.4 | Titan | 4.149 | 4.140 |
| Himalia | 27.25 | | Hyperion | 5.034 | 5.023 |
| Elara | 27.85 | 27.54 | | | 6.3 |
| (Lysithea) | (27.85) | | | | 6.65 |
| (Ananke) | (49.8) | | | | 7.00 |
| (Carme) | (53.3) | 55.46 | Iapetus | 12.09 | 12.11 |
| Pasiphae | 55.7 | | Phoebe | 43.92 | 43.85 |
| (Sinope) | (56.2) | | | | |

Table 2. Blagg's Law and the Moons of Jupiter and Saturn

## Tenikdoa, the Law of Gravity

Gurdjieff refers to gravity three times in the text of *The Tales* as a cosmic law. On the first occasion, it is while he is discussing the nature of Hanbledzoin. He writes:

> "And so, in consequence of the fact that the body Kesdjan of the being is coated with those substances which in their totality make this cosmic formation much lighter than that mass of cosmic substances which surrounds the planets and is called the planetary atmosphere, then as soon as the body Kesdjan of the being is separated from the planetary body of the being, it at once rises according to the cosmic law called 'Tenikdoa,' or as it is sometimes called the 'law of gravity,' to that sphere in which it finds the weight proper to it equally balanced and which is therefore the corresponding place of such cosmic arisings;[26]

---

[26] *The Tales*, Ch XXXVIII, Religion, p728

So, literally, Gurdjieff ascribes the rising of the body Kesdjan to a higher part of the Earth's atmosphere (in the region of the stratosphere) to the law of Tenikdoa (or gravity). The substance of the Kesdjan body is of the nature of plasma. There is a constant flow of plasma (charged ions) that rises from the surface of the Earth up to the stratosphere all the time. The body Kesdjan is probably of similar materiality and thus would also rise.

The second time Gurdjieff mentions this law is in the chapter on Religion in his criticism of spiritualism. He writes:

> "Of course, if these unfortunates would only take into consideration that according to the second-grade cosmic law called 'Tenikdoa' or 'law of gravity,' this same being-part—if in rare cases it does happen that it arises in them—instantly rises after the first Rascooarno of the being, or, as they express it, after the death of the being, from the surface of their planet; and if they understood that the explanations and proofs, given by this branch of their 'science,' of all sorts of phenomena which proceed as it were among them there thanks to those fantastic souls of theirs, were only the fruits of their idle fancy—then they would already realize that everything else proved by this science of theirs is also nothing else but Mullah Nassr Eddin's 'twaddle.'[27]

Here he repeats the idea that, in the process of the first Rascooarno (at physical death), the body Kesdjan rises high into the Earth's atmosphere. Such a relocation of this surviving body makes the idea that such entities could gather, for example, at spiritualist séances rather unlikely.

The third time he mentions this law is when discussing the degree of condensation of the air men breathe. He writes:

> "And so, the process effusion of all those substances required for the normal formation and existence of beings, which are transformed by the planet itself and which actualize the second holy force of the Sacred Triamazikamno, can proceed in the correspondingly required definite proportion only within certain limits of the atmosphere from the surface of planets because, owing to the second-grade cosmic law called Tenikdoa, or as your favorites would call it,

---

[27] The Tales, Ch XXXIX, The Holy Planet 'Purgatory', p767

*'law of gravity,' these substances cannot penetrate beyond a definite height of the atmosphere.*[28]

In this case the density of the substance is too great for it to rise above a certain level.

It is curious that in each instance Gurdjieff provides examples of the law of gravity where it causes something to rise upwards from the surface rather than to fall towards the surface. It seems to suggest that we should regard gravity as one of the forces that maintains the equilibrium (in respect of the levels of the Ray) of sun, planet or moon, rather than something that simply causes heavy objects to fall.

## The Law-of-Catching-Up

In *The Tales*, the Law-of-Catching-Up is described as complementary to the Law-of-Falling. To get an idea of the Law-of-Catching-Up it is first necessary to consider the etymology of "catching up." The modern meaning of this term comes from its figurative use in sports writing and commentary. Thus a team that is behind in a game may draw level and be said to have caught up to the other team.

However this is a relatively recent use of the term which (according to *etymonline.com*) was first recorded in 1846. The prior meaning of "catching-up" comes from early 14th century, when it meant "raising aloft" or "taking up suddenly." This meaning is still sometimes evident in current usage, when, for example, someone says that they are "caught up" in something.

So we can think of the Law-of-Catching-Up as being the law of orbiting. In *The Tales* it says:

> *"'But they could no longer fall upon their fundamental piece, because in the meantime they had come under the cosmic law called "Law-of-Catching-Up" and were entirely subject to its influence, and they would therefore now make regular elliptic orbits around their fundamental piece, just as the fundamental piece, namely, the*

---

[28] *The Tales, Ch LII. Beelzebub in America, p1050-1051*

*planet Earth, made and makes its orbit around its sun "Ors."[29]*

When we observe the cosmos, it is clearly composed of multitudes of galaxies – vast aggregations of stars, counted in the billions. Our Milky Way, for example is estimated to have up to 400 billion stars, all of which appear to be orbiting the galactic center. Suns have planets in orbit around them and most planets (in out solar system) have moons orbiting the planet.

The only planetary system we currently have detailed knowledge of is our own. We do not yet know whether other solar systems have more or less planets than ours. However, we know that there are many solar systems where large planets (often referred to as gas giants) are much closer to their sun than Jupiter is to ours. We also know that the suns, planets and moons are connected by ionic (electrical) currents and there is some kind of flow of plasma between all these bodies. However we know little more than that.

It is clear and observable that any object which enters "the sphere" of a particular sun or planet will either fall upon that sun or planet or will get caught up in an orbit around that sun or planet. If it begins to orbit such a body then it will probably do so harmoniously in accordance with Blagg's Law, as for example the planets orbit the Sun and Jupiter's, Saturns and Uranus's moons orbit their planets.

That is the harmonious order. In our solar system, it is currently violated in minor ways by the dwarf planet Pluto, whose orbit crosses that of Neptune, and also by various asteroids and comets, which intersect the orbits of planets and are destined eventually to fall onto one planet or another, or into the Sun or to be thrown out of the solar system.

If one imagines a solar system where the orbits of the planets, moons, comets and asteroids are fully harmonious, one might get the impression than nothing much will change. This is, (roughly) modern astronomy's current view of our solar system. It believes that the current harmonious behavior has persisted for over 4.5 bil-

---

[29] *The Tales, Ch IX, The Cause of the Genesis of the Moon, p83*

lion years and will continue to do so (give or take a few asteroid or comet collisions) for another 10 billion years, when the Sun expands to become a red giant.

The Work thinks otherwise. It insists that moons can evolve to become planets and planets to become suns (although such evolution is not guaranteed). The hard evidence for this perspective is discussed in *Gurdjieff's Hydrogens*.[30] The common system harmony has to adjust to accommodate the birth of new moon, the growth of planets and the creation of new solar systems.

## A Summary of Laws.

We are now in a position to summarize the relationship between Holy The Firm and the four laws that together maintain the harmony of our solar system.

1) Holy The Firm is the lowest level of the Ray of Creation, the lowest *do* which corresponds to the highest *do*. Between these manifestations of the Absolute, the megalocosmos is created. It manifests as vast number of Rays of Creation - each of which connects to a sun, planet or moon.

2) Holy The Firm provides stability to suns, planets and moons that enables the harmony of the solar system to be established.

3) Extreme circumstantial evidence suggests the orbits of planets around the sun and moons around their planets follows the pattern marked out by Blagg's Law. Currently we are not aware of any physics-based explanation as to the cause of this orbiting pattern.

4) Suns, planets and moons have atmospheres – the Sun has its heliosphere, the planets their magnetospheres and the moons have some local atmosphere. The Law-of-Falling asserts that when anything (an object of any materiality whether it is inanimate or even a cosmic arising) comes

---

[30] *Gurdjieff's Hydrogens, by R Bloor, Vol 1, Ch11, p309-315*

within the atmosphere of a sun, planet or moon, it will proceed to fall towards it.

5) However the Law-of-Catching-Up may then come into play and rather than fall onto the surface of the sun, planet or moon, it may instead orbit around it. It gets caught up in an orbit.

6) If it continues to fall, it will come under two second order laws: Litsvrtsi and Tenikdoa.

7) These two laws will ensure that the object comes in contact with objects of similar or the same materiality as itself - falling to the appropriate level but no further.

## The Trogoautoegocratic Process

We need now to include the Trogoautegocratic process into the above perspective of the Ray of Creation. Beelzebub's initial explanation of the Trogoautoegocratic process reads:

> *"... everything in the Universe, both the intentionally created and the later automatically arisen, exists and is maintained exclusively on the basis of what is called the 'common-cosmic Trogoautoego-cratic-process.'*[31]

There is no ambiguity in the words here. They insist that this process exclusively maintains everything in the Universe. Obviously this means everything at every level whether it is huge, like a galaxy, or small, like a moon, or smaller, like a human being, or even a cell in our body. The same process governs it all. The term *common-cosmic Trogoautoegocratic-process* can thus be taken to mean that this process is common to all cosmoses.

It is difficult for us to directly know the behavior of a solar system at the macrocosmic scale or the behavior of a molecule at the microcosmic scale – our time-scales are too far apart. But we know a great deal more about the behavior of our own cosmos, the human body.

---

[31] *The Tales, Ch XVII. The Arch-Absurd: According to the Assertion of Beelzebub, Our Sun Neither Lights nor Heats, p136*

It provides us with an excellent picture of a local *Trogoautoegocratic-process*.

The human body requires three foods: edibles, breath and impressions. All these three foods, entering the human cosmos from outside, are digested by being transformed. They combine with a substance of a higher vibration, in accordance with the Law of Three.

Each type of food strikes the note *do* on entry to the human body and pursues an ascending octave within the body. Most of the ingested substances are raised to higher levels in the process of digestion, although some are discarded and subsequently eliminated. Various bodily processes that utilize digested substances produce residues that are also eliminated.

So Man takes substances from outside his cosmos and eliminates substances that cannot be used by his body. All other substances created from the digestion of food fulfill specific roles in bodily or psychic processes. In all the bodily processes, all the *Trogoegoautocratic* processes, there is some organ (a purpose designed mechanism) whose job is to enable the digestion of substances – including of course, the digestion of impressions.

As regards impressions, the moving center, emotional center and intellectual center are organs for the digestion of impressions. As human beings we may identify with the working of these organs, and be proud of their capabilities, but nevertheless they are simply organs.

So the *Trogoautoegocratic* design of the body can be seen as a series of pathways or circulations for the movement of specific substances from one organ to another to enable the transformation or the use of substances within the body. We do not need to study the structure of the body for very long before we become strongly impressed with the sophistication of its design.

For example, we can consume many different substances for our first food, including any ratio you please between carbohydrates, fats and proteins, and our digestive system will process it all. It will extract everything useful it finds in what we consumed, not just lipids, sugars and amino acids, but also salts and water and it even provides food (fiber) for our symbiotic digestive bacteria.

In general, for each bodily process, there is a biological mechanism that enables the proper transformation of some substances, providing enzymes and/or hormones to enable the process. It then passes the substances on to another stage for their further transformation and use. If we think of this as a sophisticated biological factory, then we discover that in various parts of this factory there are storage points, such as the liver (for storage of glycogen and vitamins), or around most of the organs where fat is stored. At a higher level in the centers there are storage points for information (associations).

The body thus operates like a factory with strategic storage points in many places which enable it to function effectively. Aside from that, it also has a maintenance crew (the immune system) which both protects the body and maintains parts of it when they become damaged.

## Efficiency and Timing

What may not be immediately obvious about the human trogoautoegocratic process is how critical its operation is. There are many places within the human body where transformations of substances take place that enable the system to function. The right amount of particular substances has to arrive in that place in a timely manner. If it doesn't happen then the next process in sequence which depends on the substance produced by that transformation will fail.

*Throughout the system, the right quantity of the right substance must arrive in the right place at the right time.*

The factory works 24 by 7 for many decades before its deteriorates to a point where it can no longer function. It has a particular and necessary rhythm, eating perhaps three times a day, breathing every three or four seconds and receiving impressions all the time. If food is denied to it, or anything interrupts this rhythm for too long, the body dies. If any of the major organs fails to perform its function, the body dies. This is the nature of the *Trogoautoegocrat*.

So when we contemplate the meaning of the words, '*The-Harmony-of-Reciprocal-Maintenance-of-All-Cosmic-Concentrations*' it may help to think of the precision of the biological factory that we call the body. In our view it is realistic to imagine that all cosmoses are as precisely engineered as our own – at every level.

While we may not be able to see or even imagine all of the processes that keep a solar system alive, alive, it may be reasonable to consider the planets as organs. Perhaps the sun is both its heart, circulating substances we neither know nor understand, and its mind directing the activity of the planets in ways we cannot yet envisage.

We are such a small part of the solar system and our lives are far to brief for us to observe how it works. However, when we examine the harmony of our own processes, we find reason to believe that the solar system too has such a harmony. Its arrangement is not accidental.

# CHAPTER VI

# The Most High Commission

*"God is one and has three faces - think of that. One face represents the angel, the other represents the devil. The angel without the devil can do nothing. It is only together that they can do something.."*
*~ Gurdjieff*

According to Beelzebub, following the collision of Kondoor with Earth:

> … *our ENDLESSNESS was also immediately informed of this general cosmic misfortune.*

> *"In consequence of this report, a whole commission consisting of Angels and Archangels, specialists in the work of World-creation and World-maintenance, under the direction of the Most Great Archangel Sakaki, was immediately sent from the Most Holy Sun Absolute to that solar system 'Ors.' 'The Most High Commission came to our planet Mars since it was the nearest to the planet Earth and from this planet of ours began its investigations.*[32]

## The Most Great Archangel Sakaki

Archangel Sakaki directs the Most High Commission. He is referred to in the above excerpt as *Most Great* and elsewhere as *Great*.

---

[32] *The Tales, Ch IX, The Cause of the Genesis of the Moon, p82*

Subsequently we learn that Sakaki's status was later raised and he became *one of the four Quarter-Maintainers of the whole Universe.*[33]

The etymology of the name Sakaki is surprising to say the least. The name splits into *Sak* and *kaki* (in the original Russian it was written *Cakkaki*). The Russian *cak* translates to the English "sack," the German *sack* and the French *sac*. It clearly means sack. The Russian *kaki* translates to "shit." This word is also common across multiple languages. The Greek *kakos* means "bad," from which we get the English "cacophony." "Cack" is English slang for "shit." The Latin verb *cacare* means "to defecate" from which comes the French *caca* meaning "shit."

In conclusion, the name Sakaki means "bag of shit."

## *His Measurability Archangel Algamatant*

Archangel Agamatant is the other Archangel on the commission who is mentioned in the text. He is referred to by the titles: Great Arch-Engineer of the Universe, Arch-Engineer, Pantemeasurability and His Measurability.

These titles clearly imply that Algamatant possesses a specific role and skill set. The title Pantemeasurability is one of Gurdjieff's invented words composed from *panta* (Greek for "always") and *measurability* – meaning "always able to measure."

Finally we can consider the name *Algamatant*. This breaks into three parts: *alga, mat* and *ant*. The *ant* is probably the "ant" in "debutant," indicating "the one doing something."

The *mat* is probably from the English "mate" meaning "associate, fellow, or comrade;" from late 14c. Cognate with German *maat* "mate" and Dutch *maat* "partner, colleague, friend." Meaning "one of a wedded pair" is attested from 1540s. There is also "mating," as in "sexual reproduction." Originally from Greek, meaning "fits with" or "similar to."

---

[33] *The Tales, Ch IX, The Cause of the Genesis of the Moon, p89*

The *alga* is more familiar in its plural, *algae*. They are simple, non-flowering, and typically aquatic plants that include both seaweeds and many single-celled forms. Algae contain chlorophyll. This derives from the Latin *alga* for "seaweed."

Putting this all together Algamatant could mean "one who is an associate of algae."

## The Angel Looisos

Gurdjieff assigns Looisos the titles: Chief-Common-Universal-Arch-Chemist-Physicist, Arch-Chemist-Physicist and His Conformity. Clearly this angel is skilled both in physics and chemistry in some way. Looisos is initially an Angel who later becomes an Archangel – although Beelzebub provides no explanation of why his status rose.

The name Looisos breaks up into the two morphemes *Loo*, and *isos*. The *Loo* is probably the English slang word for a toilet. That slang word derives from the French expression *lieu d'aisance* (place of ease) that was adopted from the French by British soldiers during the First World War.

The second of these morphemes, *isos*, is almost certainly Greek meaning "equal to." We find this, for example, in the English word "isosceles," referring to a triangle that has two sides of equal length.

Thus Looisos' name means "equivalent to a toilet."

## Within The Human Cosmoses

We can view the story of the Kondor's collision with Earth as happening to the solar system, disturbing its cosmic harmony, leading to the formation of a moon which orbits Earth – and another body, Anulios, whose orbit about the Earth is not known.

Alternatively we can view Kondoor as a sperm which impregnates an ovum, disturbing the cosmic harmony of that body and leading to the creation of an embryo (the Moon). If we consider this second scenario, then the names and titles of these angels and archangels suddenly make perfect sense.

Sakaki is an organ of the body – the large intestine, a container of excrement or "bag of shit." This organ/archangel will be obliged to make adjustments in its activity to accommodate the disturbance to the cosmic harmony caused by the pregnancy.

Aside from storing fecal matter the large intestine absorbs water and salts from the digestive residues. It also completes the digestive process, producing among other things, B vitamins and vitamin K.

Algamatant is the ileum or small intestine – the container of a vast population of bacteria (generally over 500 species in a population estimated in the trillions). Algamatant thus earns his name and he also earns his titles: Arch-Engineer and Pantemeasurability.

The genius of the ileum becomes clear when you investigate its digestive activity. Algamatant is an accomplished chemical engineer – mixing all the required enzymes in the exact (measured) quantities with the partly digested food (chyme) that enters it from the stomach.

He is also a physical engineer. The peristaltic activity all along his 10-15 foot length mixes the chyme with enzymes and other substances from the pancreas and gall bladder and the vast local population of bacteria. Chyme will contain chunks of food not fully mashed up by the teeth and Algamatant has to gradually atomize through a process of physical and chemical activity.

He slowly advances the semi-fluid mass of chyme forwards to the point where nutrients can be absorbed into the blood stream or the lymph system. The nutrients pass through the walls of the ileum leaving behind what cannot be digested, including fiber for the local bacteria.

The digestive process is astonishingly sophisticated. It is no exaggeration to refer to the Archangel who presides over it as an Arch-Engineer.

We noted the required efficiency of the human *Trogoautoegocrat* in the previous chapter. In that light, we can only marvel at Algamatant who is charged with providing the right amount of nutrients to the rest of the body from whatever you eat – almost any combination of meat, fish, crustaceans, plant life, minerals in solid or liquid form.

## Looisos is The Womb

Looisos, also an organ of the body, is the womb. It is "equivalent to a toilet" in the sense that when it doesn't contain an embryo it is an organ of excretion that works on a lunar cycle. Indeed it could be said to act as an organ of excretion not just for the woman whose organ it is, but also by poxy for her sexual partner if she has one.

Looisos' titles: Chief-Common-Universal-Arch-Chemist-Physicist, Arch-Chemist-Physicist and His Conformity are appropriate to the womb's function of nurturing the embryo/fetus and ultimately giving birth.

The womb provides the substances required by the fertilized egg initially through the lining of the womb and subsequently through the placenta and umbilical chord. In that respect it is a chemist organizing food to pass to the fetus. In respect of pushing the baby down the birth canal and into the world it is an expert physicist.

As regards the title His Conformity, the etymology of "conform" is as follows:

**conform (v.)** mid-14c., *confourmen*, "be obedient (to God), comply*," from Old French *conformer* "conform (to), agree (to), make or be similar, be agreeable" (13c.) and directly from Latin *conformare* "to fashion, to form, to shape; educate; modify,' from assimilated form of *con (com)*" together + *formare* "to form."

The title accords with the role of Looisos in service to the cosmos of which it is part and its influence on the growth of the fetus.

## Pregnancy and Birth

It is Algamatant who informs Beelzebub about the collision of the comet Kondoor with Earth. He completes his explanation with the following words:

*"'Glory to Chance...' concluded His Pantemeasurability, 'the harmonious general-system movement was not destroyed by all this, and the peaceful existence of that system "Ors" was soon re-established.'*

*"But nevertheless, my boy, this Most High Commission, having then calculated all the facts at hand, and also all that might happen in the future, came to the conclusion that although the fragments of the planet Earth might maintain themselves for the time being in their existing positions, yet in view of certain so-called 'Tastartoonarian-displacements' conjectured by the Commission, they might in the future leave their position and bring about a large number of irreparable calamities both for this system 'Ors' and for other neighboring solar systems.*[34]

Viewing this from the human cosmos, an egg has been fertilized and a new cosmic arising is now lodged in the womb.

The High Commission was aware of what might happen in the future, and thought it likely that the fragments of the planet would maintain themselves for a while in their existing positions. However they conjecture that, due to *Tastartoonarian-displacements* they might leave their positions and bring about calamities both for the system Ors and other neighboring solar systems.

The *Tastartoonarian-displacements* are, most likely, the contractions of the womb that take place in giving birth or during a miscarriage. We have not managed to unravel the derivation of the word *Tastartoonarian*, because we are unsure of the meaning of the syllable *tar*. The morpheme *tas* means "to pant" in Turkish, *toon* means "home" in Armenian and *arian* is a genetive suffix (as in vegetarian). This suggests displacements of the embryo or fetus from the womb possibly via panting, i.e., a miscarriage or birth.

## Algamatant, Sakaki and Looisos During Pregnancy

The three angelic members of the most high commission, Algamatant, Sakaki and Looisos are the three organs most affected by pregnancy.

---

[34] *The Tales, Ch IX, The Cause of the Genesis of the Moon, p82*

70

Because of pregnancy Looisos' behaviour needs to change. His domain (the womb) needs to expand in size as the fetus develops. He will increase the flow of blood with all its nutrients to the placenta that he allows to develop so that the fetus is nourished. He will form a mucus plug in the cervix to protect the womb and its contents from infections and he prepares for the exertion of pushing the fetus down the birth canal into the world by activating the appropriate muscles.

Algamatant and Sakaki are unavoidably involved because now they have to feed two beings rather than one. To this end, both of them increase their nutrient absorption rates.

Algamatant increases the surface area of the small intestine with the growth of villi and microvilli. He slows down the peristaltic contractions of the small intestine allowing more time for the absorption of nutrients into the blood stream. This behaviour will be regulated by the hormones estrogen and progesterone which influence both the movement of the small intestine and the secretion of digestive enzymes. The blood supply to the small intestine is also increased to support growth and activity.

Sakaki is responsible for absorbing water and electrolytes from undigested food material that passes into the large intestine and this activity is boosted during pregnancy. Like Algamatant, Sakai slows the intestine's normal peristaltic action. The hormones progesterone and relaxin help to regulate the large intestine's activity during pregnancy. A common negative consequence of this change is constipation and hemorrhoids.

For both Algamatant and Sakaki there is also a change in the behavior of the community of microorganisms that reside in the gastrointestinal tract. Evidence suggests that the microbiome with its vast population of bacteria helps to maintain both the health of the mother and the fetus.

# The Gut-Brain Axis

In *The Tales* Beelzebub recounts the story of the monk Brother Asiman who attempted to discover a chemical preparation which his fellow monks could take that would allow them to survive on nothing other than water. They might thus save a great deal of time in food preparation and consumption. Although he discovered a formula which almost worked, ultimately he failed. Beelzebub refers to a document from the monastery which describes this endeavor. He relates as follows:

> *"This document contained, among other things, several very interesting details about the action of this said preparation of Asiman. It was stated that when this preparation was introduced into the presence of a being, it had besides its nourishing property, a particular action upon what are called the 'wandering nerves of the stomach'; from which action not only did the need for food immediately cease in beings, but furthermore, every desire to introduce into oneself any other edible product whatsoever entirely disappeared. And if something should be forcibly introduced, it took a long time before the disagreeable sensation and state thus provoked would pass.*

Here Gurdjieff is referring to the action of this preparation on the gut-brain axis and in particular the vagus nerve. The word "vagus" comes directly from Latin and means "strolling, wandering, rambling."

The communication pathway that connects the enteric nervous system (the gut) to the central nervous system (the brain) is called the gut-brain axis. It is an aspect of physiology that is not widely known about. Here are the basic details:

- Hormones such as serotonin, ghrelin, and leptin affect both the gut and the brain and play a role in regulating appetite, mood, and other functions.

- The vagus nerve carries signals between the brain stem and the gastrointestinal tract.

- The enteric nervous system forms a network of neurons and glial cells that controls the function of the gastrointestinal tract. It can receive input from the vagus nerve and the solar plexus.

–   In *The Tales*,[35] Gurdjieff asserts that the reconciling principle (i.e. the emotional center/brain) in Man once had a particular localization in the breast, but as men changed for the worse, Nature changed the localization system of this brain into having multiple small localizations over the body with a central point in the solar plexus.

–   Gurdjieff refers to the solar plexus as the 'complex of the nodes of the sympathetic nervous system.'[36]

–   The vagus nerve provides parasympathetic[37] sensory and motor messages to many organs and structures in the thorax and abdomen, including the heart, lungs, stomach, and intestines.

–   The vagus nerve and the solar plexus, are thus complementary in their actions and influence.

## The Microbiome and Pregnancy

The term "microbiome" is generally used to describe the totality of microbes that live on and inside our bodies, the large majority of which are found within the digestive tract. Any study of our microbiome quickly reveals that it has a much greater role in our existence than we might imagine.

There are estimated to be 30 trillion cells in the human body, less than the estimated 39 trillion microbial cells (bacteria, viruses, and fungi) of the microbiome. Research suggests that there are at least 1,000 species of bacteria, collectively possessing over 3 million genes, able to produce thousands of metabolites - far more versatile than the human genome with its 23,000 or so genes. Additionally, there are estimated to be around 10,000 species of virus. The gut mi-

---

[35] *The Tales, Ch XXXIX, The Holy Planet "Purgatory", p779*
[36] *The sympathetic nervous system being the 'fight or flight' nervous system.*
[37] *The parasympathetic nervous system being the 'rest and digest' nervous system.*

crobiome is clearly a complex and diverse symbiotic ecosystem in the human body. It engages in the following activity:

- It produces neurotransmitters such as serotonin, dopamine, and GABA,[38] which are important for regulating mood, behavior, and cognitive function.
- It can interact with the immune system to modulate inflammation in the gut, which in turn can affect brain function and behavior.
- It helps maintain the integrity of the gut barrier that separates the contents of the gut from the blood stream.
- It influences the metabolism of essential nutrients, which the body cannot itself metabolize including folate (vitamin B9) and vitamin B12.
- It helps to maintain the hypothalamic-pituitary-adrenal (HPA) axis, which plays a central role in the body's response to stress.
- Its biochemical signals can regulate the growth and function of energy-producing mitochondria across many cell types, including those in fat, muscles, heart, and the brain.

In summary, the gut microbiome can communicate with the brain through various pathways, including the vagus nerve, the immune system, and the endocrine system, and it plays a vital role in regulating the gut-brain axis.

The microbial world of the gut (the associates of Algamatant) responds to pregnancy. With the onset of pregnancy the microbial population becomes more diverse and may acquire some new capabilities. The relative abundance of some bacteria that are known to be beneficial, such as lactobacilli increases.

The immune system of the gut is boosted and modified. During pregnancy, the immune system moderates its behavior in order not to attack the fetus in the womb – which is "a foreign object." The gut microbiota are believed to be involved in this immunosuppression.

---

[38] *The neurotransmitter Gamma-aminobutyric acid.*

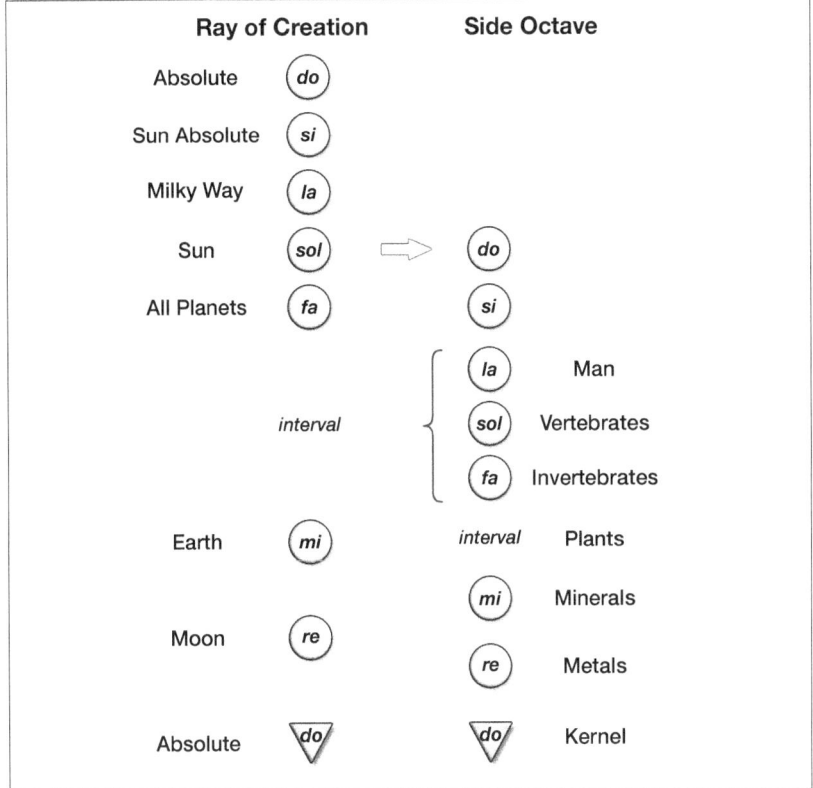

*Figure 8. The Side Octave*

During pregnancy, changes in the gut microbiome can affect the regulation of stress and anxiety, which can impact maternal and fetal health. It is possible that the food cravings that pregnant women experience relates to the microbiome (rather than the woman herself) requesting particular food via the gut-brain axis.

## Filling the *mi-fa* Interval

Now consider *Figure 8* above showing the side octave from the Sun and its role in the Ray of Creation. The Work teaches that interval between *fa* (the Planets) and *mi* (the Earth) is filled by organic life on Earth. More precisely it is filled by bacteria and plants which occupy the *mi-fa* interval in the side octave between minerals and bio-

75

logical life, on top of which lie one-brained, two-brained and three-brained beings.

Biological life (Great Nature) forms a skin over the planet Earth and, in ways that we do not entirely understand, receives the magnetic and electromagnetic radiation from the planets and passes it to the Earth. As such, organic life is a transmission station for such influences. For example, Gurdjieff describes the cosmic law of Solioonesius, caused by tensions between planets and/or suns as causing particular states in Man which can lead to aggressive behavior and war, or could alternatively be used for personal self-perfection.

## The *mi-fa* Interval in Man

If we can think the Ray of Creation of the Megalocosmos has a side-octave, then we ought to be able to view the Ray of Creation in Man as also having a side octave. The possible structure of such a side octave is illustrated in *Figure 9.*

The main point to note here is that the bacteria of the alimentary canal fulfill the same role in Man as organic life fulfills in respect of the Earth and the Planets. The *mi-fa* interval in the octave of the physical body is the point where food enters in.[39] The gut bacteria in collaboration with the enzymes and bile produced by the organism (from the mouth, stomach, small intestine, pancreas and gall bladder) help to digest food. They break down and consume fiber of various kinds, creating substances that help maintain the microbiome and assist the flow of substances through the alimentary canal in an optimum manner.

It is not our intention here to investigate this side octave in depth, just to point out its existence and the relationships between Algamatant, Sakaki and Looisos that it suggests.

In *The Tales*, Gurdjieff switches Beelzebub's focus between different cosmoses without warning the reader. In the case of a pregnant

---

[39] See In Search of the Miraculous by Peter Ouspensky, p293

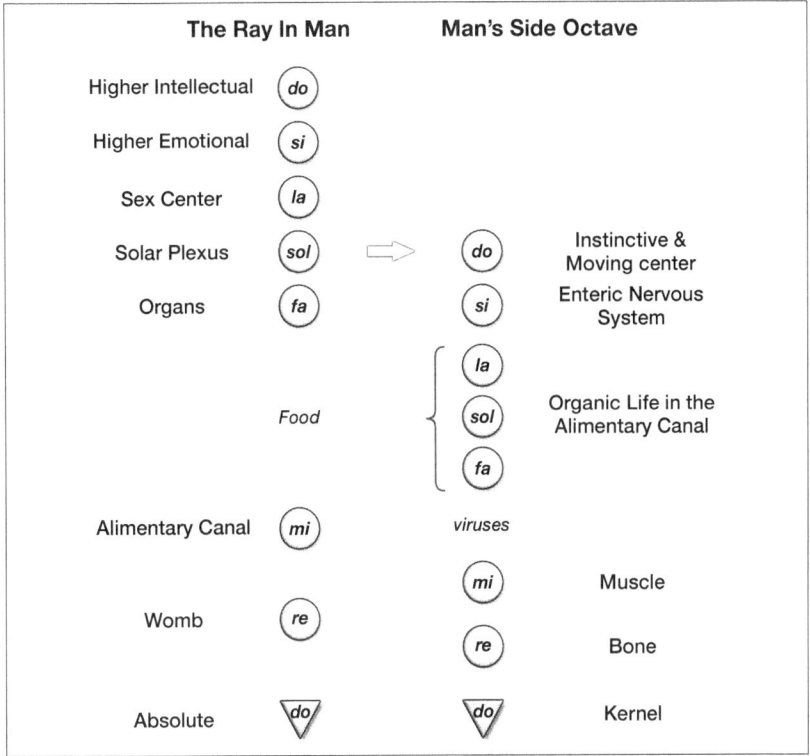

*Figure 9. Man's Side Octave*

woman, Algamatant, Sakaki and Looisos represent organs of her body, but if we consider the solar system as a cosmos, they represent something else entirely.

Theoretically, the Earth may be the abdomen of the Solar system, comprising the whole of its alimentary canal and its womb, and perhaps more. If so, Algamatant, Sakaki and Looisos are angelic characters, who watch over the Earth. Observing the genesis of the Moon, they conclude that in future the Moon might be displaced from its orbit and subsequently cause calamities for the solar system.

"*Therefore the Most High Commission decided to take certain measures to avoid this eventuality.*

"*And they resolved that the best measure in the given case would be that the fundamental piece, namely, the planet Earth, should constantly send to its detached fragments, for their maintenance, the sacred vibrations 'Askokin.'*

*"This sacred substance can be formed on planets only when both fundamental cosmic laws operating in them, the sacred 'Heptaparaparshinokh' and the sacred 'Triamazikamno,' function, as is called, 'Ilnosoparno,' that is to say, when the said sacred cosmic laws in the given cosmic concentration are deflected independently and also manifest on its surface independently – of course independently only within certain limits.*[40]

Askokin possibly means "familial love,"[41] – the love of the Earth for its child. The meaning of Ilnosoparno is clear, although its derivation is less clear.[42] In *In Search of the Miraculous* we read.

*G. returned to the enneagram many times and in various connections. "Each completed whole, each cosmos, each organism, each plant, is an enneagram," he said. "But not each of these enneagrams has an inner triangle. The inner triangle stands for the presence of higher elements, according to the scale of 'hydrogens,' in a given organism. This inner triangle is possessed by such plants, for example, as hemp, poppy, hops, tea, coffee, tobacco, and many other plants which play a definite role in the life of man. The study of these plants can reveal much for us in regard to the enneagram.*[43]

It is reasonable to conclude that the higher hydrogens referred to above are analogous to the sacred Askokin that the Moon requires from Earth and without which it will cease to grow. So the Most High Commission seeks permission from HIS ENDLESSNESS, to sanction the actualization of the *ilnosoparnian* process on Earth. We read:

*"And afterwards, when the said Sacred Individuals had obtained the sanction of HIS ENDLESSNESS for the actualization of the Ilnosoparnian process on that planet also, and when this process had been actualized under the direction of the same Great Archangel Sakaki, then from that time on, on that planet also, just*

---

[40] *The Tales, Ch IX, The Cause of the Genesis of the Moon, p84*
[41] **Ask** *in Turkish means "love," and* **kin** *means family.*
[42] **Il** *is the French pronoun, "he/she/it'," noso is Greek for illness,* **parno** *is uncertain..*
[43] *In Search of the Miraculous, p293*

*as on many others, there began to arise the 'Corresponding,' owing to which the said detached fragments exist until now without constituting a menace for a catastrophe on a great scale.[44]*

The "Corresponding" is almost certainly a major alteration to the life of Great Nature, analogous to the changes we previously discussed in respect of the cosmos of a prospective mother. In particular it requires the evolution of one-brained, two-brained and three-brained beings.

There is value in pondering the question: "what is Anulios in the cosmos of Earth?" It is a high fragment of the Earth that is maintained by energies provided by Man. Here we can only speculate as to what its orbit is – most likely it lies within the Earth's magnetosphere, but given that the higher intellectual center in Man runs on H6, we assume that the substances H12, H24 and possibly H6 itself are what mankind sends to Anulios (or Kimespai - *never allowing one to sleep in peace*).

Looking at it another way, maybe Anulios donates the higher intellectual center to Man, and reclaims it at death. Possibly it is by virtue of Anulios that messengers from above occasionally descend to Earth to benefit mankind.

---

[44] *The Tales, Ch IX, The Cause of the Genesis of the Moon, p85*

# CHAPTER VII

## Nature, Man and the Moon

*The liberation which comes with the growth of mental powers and
faculties is liberation from the moon.*
*~ Gurdjieff*

Gurdjieff describes the Moon as being the progeny of the comet Kondoor's collision with the Earth. In the cosmos of man, where the Earth represents an ovum and the comet a sperm, the Moon is the fetus. In the cosmos of the solar system, it is unlikely if not impossible, for the collision of a comet with a planet to result in anything other than the destruction of the comet and some relatively small impact damage to the surface of the planet.

Thus we have little choice but to see the text of *The Tales* as an allegory for human reproduction. This leaves us with the question:

### How was the Moon created?

Contemporary science offers multiple theories to explain the Moon's origin. One suggests that it was captured by Earth's gravitation as it flew by – at some point in the very distant past. Another suggests that the Earth and Moon formed together as a double system, from the primordial gas cloud circling the Sun. The currently favored theory is that Earth initially had no moon, but a collision with an early "protoplanet" caused the ejection of a great deal of material from

Earth, with some of it forming the Moon and the rest drifting off into space.

Because Theia was the mother of Selene, the Moon goddess, in Greek myth, astronomers named this theoretical protoplanet Theia. A big problem with this theory arises in trying to explain what happened to Theia after the collision. No evidence of its existence has been found within the solar system, so the presumption must be that it either drifted away beyond the heliopause or it disintegrated and gradually fell onto the Sun and onto other planets.

There are different collision opinions, too; one suggests that Theia gave the Earth a glancing blow and another that it hit the Earth head-on. The theory has been modeled using computer simulations. However, as we have no data about what happens when planets collide (if they ever do), the simulations are, at best, speculative guesses that prove nothing.

Also, if it is true that a planetary collision is required to give rise to a large moon, then there must have been a good many such collisions to create Saturn's large moon, Titan and the four large moons of Jupiter (Ganymede, Callisto, Io and Europa), three of which are larger than Earth's moon.

## The Distinct Difference in Astronomical Models

The standard astronomical model of the origin of the solar system and its development is completely at variance with the model introduced by Gurdjieff. We illustrate the disparity in *Table 3* on the following page.[45]

The contemporary astronomical model theorizes that all the elements heavier than iron which are found on planets are formed in supernovas and scattered into clouds of dust from which planets form by accretion. However, following this birth from a cloud of dust, the planets remain roughly the same size in perpetuity. If anything subsequently occurs to the planet (collisions or disintegration

---

[45] *For a more complete explanation see Gurdjieff's Hydrogens, Vol 1, by Robin Bloor*

| Modern Astronomy | The Work |
|---|---|
| Stars form by aggregation of dust at the center of a dust cloud. | Stars are created by Law of Three interactions during The Creation or by planetary evolution thereafter. |
| Once formed Stars go through a life-cycle that begins with internal nuclear fusion and ends either in a supernova or in the formation of a white dwarf. | A star can form from a planet growing and eventually becoming incandescent. |
| Planets form by aggregation of dust from around a star. | Planets form directly from stars by Law of Three interactions. |
| Once formed the size of a planet does not vary significantly. | Planets can grow to become suns or decline to become lifeless, eventually being absorbed by another planet, or star. |
| Moons may be captured by gravitational pull, or formed by accretion at the same time as their parent planet – or formed by a major impact – or by fission when material is ejected from the parent planet. They do not grow. | Moons form directly from planets by Law of Three interactions. They grow and evolve or involve (i.e. fail). |

*Table 3. A Distinct Difference in Astronomical Models*

into asteroids) it is assumed to have happened in the early days after planetary birth.

The question naturally arises as to how moons form and there are four theories, as shown in the above table. However, when it comes to the Earth's own moon, there is evidence that can be analyzed.

## The Moon is a Child of the Earth

The Moon rocks that NASA's astronauts retrieved provide us with credible evidence that the Moon is indeed a child of the Earth – extensive chemical analyses have concluded that the Moon it has similar geological "DNA" to Earth. This provides the best and, as far as we are aware, the only evidence of the Moon's origin.

The isotopic signatures of lunar rocks are almost identical to those of Earth's igneous rocks. They differ significantly from the results obtained by analyzing meteorites (rocks that landed on earth that originated from elsewhere). A study published in 2013 indicated that water in lunar magma is almost the same in isotopic composition as water found in Earth magma. Other published analyses reach the same conclusion: that the rocky surface of the Moon derives from material that originated on Earth. The only observed difference is that lunar rocks seem to have more aluminum and titanium, which may be due to local effects occurring over millions of years either to the Earth or the Moon.

Given this information, the protoplanet collision theory is difficult to defend. If there ever was a Theia, lunar rocks ought to show some evidence of material from Theia. The likelihood of Theia having an identical isotopic signature to the Earth is vanishingly small. The only area of doubt surrounds the question of whether rocks from other sites on the Moon might reveal a different composition.

## The Birth of Suns and Planets

In *Gurdjieff's Hydrogens*[46] we presented an alternative theory concerning the birth of suns, and planets, based on the Electric Universe model – a fairly recent set of theories, which have become increasingly credible with time and which have many points of agreement with objective science as taught by Gurdjieff.

This theory rejects the idea that the determining factor in the operation of the Universe is gravity and instead asserts that the dominat-

---

[46] *Gurdjieff's Hydrogens, Vol 1, by Robin Bloor p285*

ing factor at the large scale (and in fact at all scales) is the electro-magnetic force. This would not seem a particularly radical idea were it not that Einstein's theory of gravity has long been the primary pillar of astronomical and astrophysics dogma.

This theory became high fashion long before anyone had gathered much data about the nature of space. The assumption had been that space was empty, except for the constant passage through it of electromagnetic waves. As a consequence, early space shots made no attempt to detect plasma (electrically charged atoms and particles) because, at the time, their presence in the fabric of space was never suspected.

However, it has gradually become clear that the Universe is awash with plasma, to the point where recent estimates suggest that the Universe is 99.9% plasma. At the macro scale almost everything is electric: comets, the atmospheres of planets, the heliosphere of the Sun which surrounds the solar system, and the extensive electric clouds that surround galaxies. Galaxies are linked together by a vast web of electrical flows (Birkeland currents).

The force of electromagnetism is $10^{36}$ times stronger than the force of gravity – vastly stronger, almost inconceivably stronger. It is the force that determines the circular motion of galaxies. (Attempts to explain gravity as the responsible force have failed completely.) Most likely electromagnetism is the force that determines the motion of all heavenly bodies to some degree. However, exactly how electromagnetic forces operate at large scale is not yet fully understood.

The Electric Universe model aligns with the idea that suns give birth to planets and planets give birth to moons. The idea that moons can become planets and that planets can become suns, as suggested by Gurdjieff, also fits this theory There is very credible evidence that the Earth has increased in size in the past and may still be growing.[47]

---

[47] *Gurdjieff's Hydrogens, Vol 1, by Robin Bloor p309-317*

The Electric Universe theory asserts that new stars and planets are born when a supernova or a nova occurs. A study of stars reveals that many stars are binary or even triple star systems. If you consider just the 60 nearest stars then 61% of them are part of dual or triple star systems. Such systems are common.

The evidence suggests that star can undergo a fission process similar in concept to cell division. Donald Scott in his book about the Electric Universe explains the process as follows:

> "Internal electrostatic forces prevent stars from collapsing gravitationally and occasionally cause them to 'give birth' by electrical fissioning to form companion stars and gas giant planets. Sudden brightening or a nova outburst marks such an event. That explains why stars commonly have partners and why most of the giant planets so far detected closely orbit their parent star.
>
> The cause of stellar fissioning may also be external. We have said a star is a sphere of plasma. As such, the ions and electrons within it have (random) thermal velocities. If the incoming electric current density increases so that the drift velocity of those particles exceeds the value of the thermal velocity, this produces a double layer (DL). The DL may move down into the plasma (into the star). At this position the DL can act much like a membrane that divides a biological cell. If the current density increases to too high a value, the DL may a explode, splitting the star into two or more parts.[48]

So the theory is that a star forms a series of double layers of plasma that act as membranes. One membrane surrounds the star while another descends into the interior and divides it into two. The exterior membrane becomes increasingly unstable and explodes.

There is a burst of gamma-rays, then an explosion of visible light. It leaves a plasma cloud (or nebula) and two stars rather than a single star in its wake. The two stars are wrapped in plasma double layers, as shown in *Figure 10*. They have different surface current density, temperature, luminosity, and spectral type to the parent star they emerged from, indicating a loss of energy.

---

[48] *The Interconnected Cosmos by Donald E. Scott*

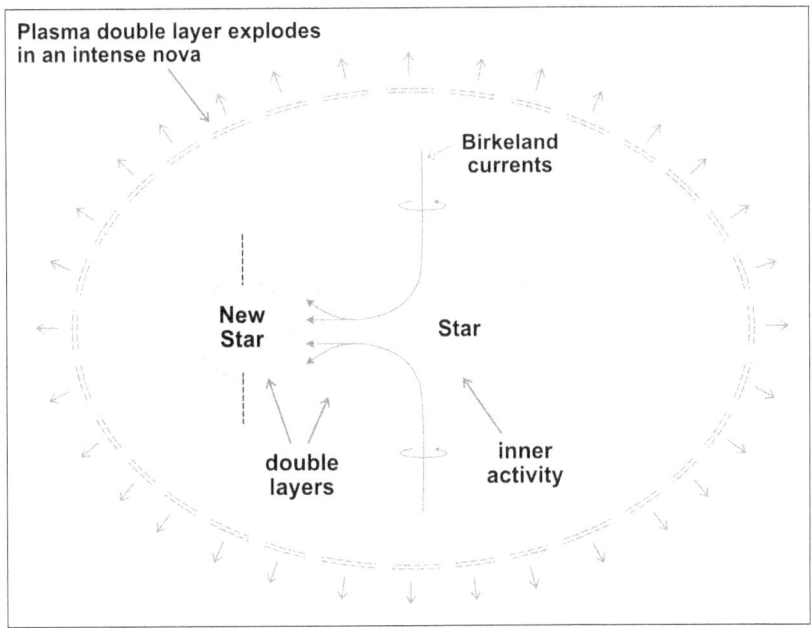

*Figure 10. The Birth of a Star*

When a sphere splits into two smaller ones, although the volume of material remains the same, their combined surface area is greater than that of the original sphere. By splitting a star in this way, the electrical current density of the total surface reduces. If the resulting two spheres are of equal size, the increase in surface area is 26%.

The Crab Nebula provides an excellent picture of the aftermath of a supernova – one that Chinese astronomers observed in 1054 AD. At the center of the nebula is a pulsar (CM Tauri) that pulses 30 times per second. It has a small companion star that is 1500 AU distant from it.

Lesser novas likely create planets – gas giants or even smaller bodies. The birth of the Moon may have involved this kind of electric fissioning process. It seems tangentially related that when a human or animal sperm fertilizes an ovum, there is a flash of light.[49]

---

[49] Link: https://www.sciencealert.com/scientists-just-captured-the-actual-flash-of-light-that-sparks-when-sperm-meets-an-egg

Readers who wish to study the astronomical perspective offered by the Electric Universe theories may want to read the books already mentioned. There are also other books available.[50] Aside from those sources there are many videos to watch on Youtube (look for videos entitled *The Thunderbolts Project*, particularly those presented by Wallace Thornhill or Michael Clarage).

## The Moon in The Ray of Creation

In describing the Ray of Creation, Gurdjieff likens it to a tree with many branches and twigs.*[51] If you think of the Absolute as the tree's trunk, each lower note in the Ray represents a branching. At the bottom of the Ray are the Earth and Moon. The Moon is the growing end of a twig that sprouted from the Earth.

The energy that the Moon needs to grow comes from the Earth. It is created on the Earth by the joint action of the Sun, the other Planets, and the Earth itself. This energy is collected and stored in a large accumulator – organic life on Earth. In that respect, all biological life serves to feed the Moon. There is a mutual dependency in this. Gurdjieff said that without organic life, the Moon would die, and conversely, if there were no Moon, organic life would cease.

There is some circumstantial evidence for this. Space exploration has found no evidence of organic life on any other planet in the solar system (beyond bacterial life, which we cannot discount). Nevertheless, there may once have been organic life on Mars. There is a great deal of evidence of sedimentary layers in the rock on Mars, which only occur where there is an abundance of flowing water. It is difficult to imagine the creation of significant amounts of sedimentary rock without assistance from organic life. Mars does not have a substantial moon. Its two satellites, Phobos and Deimos, are respectively 13.8 miles (22.2 km) and 7.8 miles (12.6 km) in diameter. They are more akin to orbiting asteroids than moons. It may be, then, that Mars once nursed a moon, but it failed. Without a robust

---

[50] *Including: The Electric Universe by Wallace Thornhill and David Talbott and A Beginner's View of Our Electric Universe by Tom Findlay*

[51] *In Search of the Miraculous by P D Ouspensky, p134*

magnetosphere to shield it from the solar winds, Mars currently appears to be losing its atmosphere. It appears to be a failing planet

We can think of the Moon as an embryo that is gradually growing. It exhibits no movement of its own – it does not spin on its axis. The moment this happens may correspond to the fetal quickening. If so, then calculations suggest that the Moon will need to move twice as far from the Earth as it currently is for that to occur.

## The Moon's Atmosphere

Currently, the Moon has a very thin atmosphere. At sea level on Earth, there are about $10^{19}$ molecules per cc, whereas, on the Moon's surface, the lunar atmosphere has less than $10^6$ molecules per cc. That lack of density is similar to the Earth's atmosphere 300-400 km above sea level at the outermost fringes of our atmosphere. Nevertheless it is an atmosphere which is significantly denser than the solar wind that pervades the space between planets, which has just a few protons per cc.

Three noble gases, argon, helium, and neon, dominate the Moon's atmosphere. There are also traces of hydrogen, ammonia, methane, carbon dioxide, carbon monoxide, nitrogen, sodium, and potassium. Lunar soil contains water in very small quantities. Scientists suspect that there is ice in craters at the Moon's poles. There may be an extremely weak water cycle that transports water to the poles.

The supposed causes for the Moon's atmosphere are:

– high energy photons and solar wind particles ejecting atoms from the lunar surface.

– evaporation of surface material.

– chemical reactions between the solar wind and lunar surface material.

– material thrown out by comet and meteoroid impact.

– gases released from chemical interactions below the Moon's surface.

– electrostatically raised dust.

Thin atmospheres exist elsewhere in the solar system: on Mercury, the larger moons of other planets, and large asteroids. Such atmospheres are unable to retain lighter gases. Hydrogen and helium tend to escape into space.

*Planetary Atmosphere*

There is a distinct difference between the atmosphere of the Moon and that of a typical planet. Most planets have a self-created magnetosphere. The Moon does not. When it lies outside the Earth's magnetosphere, the solar wind from the Sun induces currents in the body of the Moon, which in turn generate a "magnetosphere."

*Figure 11* above illustrates Earth's magnetosphere. It shields the Earth's atmosphere and all biological life from the impact of the solar wind, solar radiation, and cosmic rays.

The boundary and the outermost layer of the magnetosphere meet the solar wind head-on, deflecting it around the Earth and slowing it down. The region between the bow shock and the magnetopause is called the magnetosheath. It consists primarily of solar wind intermixed with small amounts of magnetosphere plasma (charged particles). In this region, the direction and magnitude of the magnetic field vary erratically.

The magnetopause is the magnetosphere's boundary where the repellant pressure from the Earth's magnetic field balances the pressure of the solar wind. It's size and shape fluctuates in harmony with the solar wind. A small stream of solar wind penetrates the magnetopause at the points labeled "cusp," descending into the Earth's atmosphere near the poles. This energetic input gives rise to the northern lights and the southern lights.

The magnetosphere is not at all spherical; rather, it is a very elongated malformed spheroid extending away from the Sun. Earth's Sun-facing bow shock is a mere 56,000 miles from Earth and about 11 miles thick. The magnetopause below it is just a few hundred miles above Earth's surface. However, on Earth's nightside, the mag-

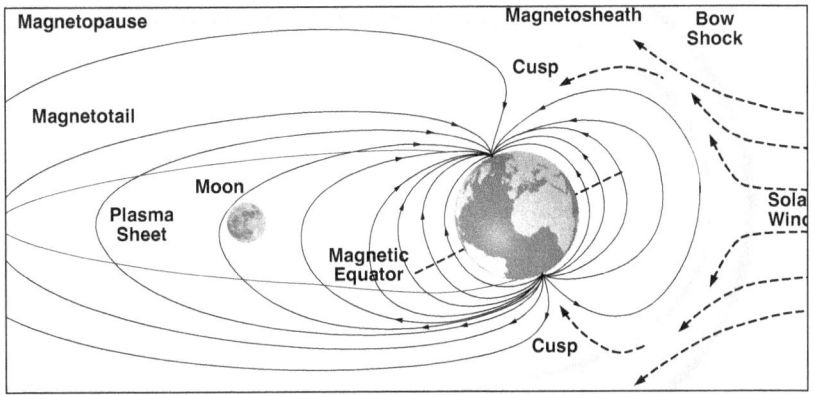

*Figure 11. The Earth's Magnetosphere*

netotail extends 3,900,000 miles from Earth, a distance that is roughly 15 times as great as the orbit of the Moon. Within it, extending in the same direction, is a plasma sheet, a denser and hotter plasma region than is present in the other regions of the magnetotail. The orbit of the Moon passes through this plasma sheet.

The local magnetic field of the Moon is extremely weak. Measurements suggest that the local magnetization is almost entirely crustal in origin. Large impact events could be the cause of the local magnetic fields. The largest crustal magnetizations are near the antipodes of the moon's "giant impact basins." Their formation may be the cause of those magnetic fields.

## Feeding The Moon

It is clear that if organic life feeds the Moon – in the sense of providing substances to it – it must do so, physically, by sending it plasma-based substances. These could be substances with the density of H96, H48, and H24. These Hydrogens are energies of the psyche. They are almost certainly negatively charged ionic matter. Such substances will naturally find their way to the Moon by ionic flow – electromagnetic attraction.

We can conceive of this as follows. When a man or other animal dies, its corpse begins to behave differently at the microbiological level. The immune system, which had previously governed and policed the microbiological world, has vanished (departed). The internal temperature of the body is no longer controlled and bacteria – agents of deconstruction – multiply. The skin ruptures allowing the entry of air and more bacteria and even insects. The corpse becomes food and gradually releases various useful substances into the environment that can be nutrients for local life-forms.

However, while alive, the being also used and maintained some quantity of higher Hydrogens. H96 is the energy of the immune system, and more vivifying Hydrogens (H48, H24 and H12) are the substances of the psyche.

In respect of Man, we can think of personality, which includes H48 and H24, as food for the Moon. The personality forms through imitation, education, movies, radio, and books, all the hypnotic influences of life. They furnish the mechanical backbone of the personality, furnishing different behaviors for different situations, evoked by everyday impressions and frequently repeated.

The personality's role is to shield essence – acting as a kind of skin. Its mechanics are like the dead skin covering the body that acts as a barrier to external pathogens. As the epidermis cells (the outer layer of skin) mature, they produce keratin, a fibrous, waterproof compound. The body also uses keratin to create nails and hair and (in other life-forms) claws, horns, hooves, scales, shells, and beaks. By the time epithelial cells reach the skin's surface, they are dead, scale-like structures that form an organic barrier to the outer world. When ruptures of the skin occur, epithelial scar tissue grows over the wound.

In a similar manner, the personality acts as an automatic barrier to deflect external influences from reaching essence. We tend to identify with the personality despite its defects (vanity, lies, deceit, imagination, negative emotions, etc.), which we rarely observe. We believe that the mechanical (dead) personality is "I." Just like the surface of the skin, our usual behavior is to continually renew our personality, which we do through repeated behavior. In those who work on themselves, essence may learn from personality, but in others, it rarely happens.

In *In Search of the Miraculous*,[52] Gurdjieff relates the Moon's feeding to the death of organic life. He says that everything living provides some of the energy that animated it in life to the Moon. He refers to this energy as the "souls" of living things, attracted to the Moon as if by an electromagnet.

In respect of men, he suggests that even a certain amount of consciousness and memory goes to the Moon, where it finds itself under ninety-six orders of Laws, in the conditions of mineral life, from which there is no escape except by the evolution of the Moon itself. In some way, personality and some of the structures that support it go to the Moon.

In *The Tales*, Beelzebub refers to a conversation with Archangel Looisos in respect of feeding the Moon, saying:

> *"And further, His Highness also explained that this cosmic substance, the Sacred Askokin, exists in general in the Universe chiefly blended with the sacred substances 'Abrustdonis' and 'Helkdonis,' and hence that this sacred substance Askokin in order to become vivifying for such a maintenance must first be freed from the said sacred substances Abrustdonis and Helkdonis.*

> *"To tell the truth, my boy, I did not at once clearly understand all that he then said, and it was only later that I came to understand it all clearly, when, during my studies of the fundamental cosmic Laws, I learned that these sacred substances Abrustdonis and Helkdonis are just those substances by which the higher being-bodies of three-brained beings, namely, the body Kesdjan and the body of the Soul, are in general formed and perfected; and when I learned that the separation of the sacred Askokin from the said sacred substances proceeds in general when the beings on whatever planet it might be transubstantiate the sacred substances Abrustdonis and Helkdonis in themselves for the forming and perfecting of their*

---

[52] *In Search of the Miraculous by P D Ouspensky, p85*

*higher bodies, by means of conscious labors and intentional sufferings.*[53]

Put simply, the Moon feeds on Askokin, which comes from the substances Abrustdonis and Helkdonis, which Men can use to perfect their higher bodies. There is a distinction between the substances that Man can provide and those that the rest of nature can provide. Men who are trying to perfect themselves generate Askokin directly and thus feed the Moon while alive. All other men feed the Moon in the process of Rascooarno, the breaking up of their body when they die. Man is the only type of being on Earth that can feed the specific energies that come from intellectual activity.

### The Magnetotail and The Moon

For there to be a feeding process between the Earth and the Moon, there must be a connecting structure roughly corresponding to a placenta through which nutrients pass. The nutrients coming from organic life comprise substances that correspond to Hydrogens H96 or higher.

It is likely then that the "placenta and umbilical chord" between Earth and Moon is the Earth's Magnetotail. Such materials, less dense than the air, naturally rise upwards. They carry a negative charge, as does the Earth's surface. Retaining their negative charge, such substances may rise to the top of the ionosphere and enter the magnetosphere.

At maximum, Earth's exosphere stretches approximately 190,000 kilometers (120,000 miles) towards the Moon and makes no contact. However, the Earth's magnetotail extends far beyond the orbit of the Moon. The Moon passes through it, spending about six days in every lunar month inside it.

The electrical state of the Moon varies according to its orbital position. When it is outside the Earth's magnetotail, the weak magnetosphere bestowed upon it by the solar wind insulates it. We suspect that the protection this affords the Moon is critical to it retaining its

---

[53] *The Tales, Ch XLIII, Beelzebub's Opinion of War, p1106*

negative charge. If it did not have a magnetosphere at all, direct interaction with the positive ions of the solar wind would cause it to become electrically neutral.

When the Moon enters the magnetotail, the solar wind is deflected away, and the plasma sheet within the Earth's magnetotail takes over. The plasma sheet is in a constant state of motion and hotter (i.e., more energetic) than the solar wind. During the six days as the Moon passes through the magnetotail, the magnetosphere's plasma sheet sweeps across it many times, with encounters lasting anywhere from minutes to hours or even days. Electrons pepper the Moon's surface, increasing the Moon's negative charge. On the Moon's Sun-facing side, the sunlight counteracts this. Photons of ultraviolet light displace electrons from the surface. Thus the nightside of the Moon is negatively charged compared to the dayside.

NASA's Lunar Prospector spacecraft, which orbited the Moon in 1998-99, gathered the best data we currently have about magneto-tail crossings. During some crossings, it detected significant changes in the lunar nightside voltage, typically rising from -200 V to -1000 V. In 2017,[54] Japanese researchers, analyzing data from Japan's Moon-orbiting Kaguya spacecraft, reported that oxygen ions from the Earth's atmosphere made their way to the surface of the Moon during the Moon's passage through the magnetotail.

The passage of negatively charged plasma from the Earth to the Moon is thus well established. Gurdjieff said:

> … *in relation to organic life the moon is a huge electromagnet. If the action of the electromagnet were suddenly to stop, organic life would crumble to nothing.*
>
> *"The process of the growth and the warming of the moon is connected with life and death on the earth. Everything living sets free at its death a certain amount of the energy that has 'animated' it; this energy, or the 'souls' of everything living – plants, animals, people – is attracted to the moon as though by a huge electromagnet, and brings to it the warmth and the life upon which its growth depends,*

---

[54] *Article entitled: Moon found to be periodically showered with oxygen ions from Earth*
*https://phys.org/news/2017-01-moon-periodically-showered-oxygen-ions.html*

*that is, the growth of the ray of creation.*[55]

It is during the Moon's passage through the magnetotail that the Moon behaves as an electromagnet. Outside the magnetotail, under the solar wind's direct influence, it will not attract anything from the Earth.

## The Moon's Evolution

The elliptical orbit of the Moon varies in radius between 238,900-225,700 miles (384,400-363,300 km). Laser-based measurements indicate that it is slowly receding at a rate of 1.5 inches (3.8 centimeters) per year. Models of the mutual gravitational influence suggest that the Moon's rate of recession will decrease with time. The theory is that while the Moon recedes, the Earth's spin gradually reduces, and the day gets longer. So projections suggest that the Earth and Moon will eventually find a stable orbit with the Moon and Earth locked into permanently facing each other. In theory, the Moon's orbit will then take approximately 47 (24 hour) days, and Earth's rotation will have slowed down to a single rotation taking 47 (24 hour) days. These projections are almost certainly wrong.

# The Uniqueness of the Earth's Moon

The Earth's moon is distinct from others in the solar system. All the other moons are part of moon families. Jupiter has 80 or more moons, Saturn 82 or more, Uranus 27, and Neptune 14. It appears that these planets are more mature than Earth and on their way to becoming solar systems.

Earth has one large moon with an orbital period of 27.3 days. This suggests (it seems logical) that our Moon is more mature in its development than any of these other moons, even though the Earth looks less mature than those four gas giants in respect of becoming a sun with its own solar system. That seems odd, but it's not the only thing distinctive about our moon.

---

[55] *In Search of the Miraculous by Peter Ouspensky, p85*

Due to its proximity to the Sun, Earth's moon is by far the warmest moon. Its mean temperature, $250^0$K at its equator, varies from $100^0$K, far colder than it ever gets on Earth, to $390^0$K, significantly hotter than it ever gets on Earth. It gets hot, but because of its extremely thin atmosphere, it cannot retain the heat.

The high temperature explains the Moon's lack of ice. Almost all other large moons in the solar system (Io is the exception), have substantial amounts of water ice on their surface. If they were hotter, the ice would become water and then water vapor and, for a moon with a thin atmospheres, the water would be split by radiation into hydrogen and oxygen, with the hydrogen escaping from the atmosphere. Much of the water would be lost.

The other distinctive feature of our moon is that it orbits a planet which has a vibrant biosphere. As yet, there is no evidence of any biological life anywhere else in the solar system. Although it is highly likely that there is life at the bacterial level on other planets (perhaps even all planets) there is no evidence anywhere of a significant biosphere.

We can only study one solar system (its planets and its moons) to theorize as to exactly what path the evolution of a moon follows (or even what path the evolution of a planet follows). So, beyond the scant theory that Gurdjieff provides us with, we cannot say for certain that what the life-cycle of a planet or a moon is.

Nevertheless, given the current state of astronomical concepts and knowledge associated with the Electric Universe theory, the assertion that the Earth and the Moon are growing and that life on Earth provides food for the Moon is, in our view, credible.

# Gurdjieff and Kundabuffer

# CHAPTER VII

## The Abnormal Conditions of Being-Existence

*"Divide in yourself the mechanical from the conscious, see how little there is of the conscious – how seldom it works."*
*~ P. D. Ouspensky*

Beelzebub repeatedly points out that there are two causes that are responsible for the sorry state of mankind. On the one hand are the "abnormal conditions of being-existence" established by our own actions, or those of our ancestors. On the other hand there are influences that we could not avoid as they are consequences of the properties of the organ Kundabuffer.

Many readers of *The Tales* will have given little thought to the phrase "the abnormal conditions of being-existence" – a phrase which is sometimes accompanied by its companion phrase "established by them themselves," clearly indicating that the fault for this falls on humanity.

The most important word in this oft-repeated phrase is "being." This word is used by Gurdjieff as an adjective (i.e. as a noun adjunct) on numerous occasions, in over a hundred different ways. For example, we encounter: being-ableness, being-Aimnophnian-mentation, being-associations, being-conscience, being-data, being-function, being-love-of-knowledge, being-notion, being-organ, being-Partkdolg-duty, being-sane-mentation, being-self-shame, being-wish and inner-being-experiencing – to mention just a few.

To skip over these words and not ponder their meaning, understandable though it may be, given our tendency to mechanical reading, is to ignore their meaning entirely.

With the phrase "the abnormal conditions of being-existence," Gurdjieff cannot possibly mean "the abnormal conditions of existence." The conditions of human existence vary widely across the globe and it is difficult to generalize about them in any way. However, with the word "being-existence" the phrase acquires an entirely different meaning.

A possible explanation as to why Gurdjieff uses the word "being" in this way is that the Ray of Creation, which spans the Megalocosmos, is a *scale of being* with each point on the Ray above the Moon representing an increase in being. People who are attracted to The Work are generally those who have a wish to increase their level of being. As such they are, by definition, concerned with their being-existence.

Others who have no interest in a spiritual path may have no reason to be concerned about the current conditions of man's being-existence, and even if they do – as an example, consider someone who passionately believes we could better exploit the minerals wealth of the Earth – it is not the "being-existence" of mankind that concerns them. They may even regard the current conditions of man's existence as satisfactory and not in the least bit abnormal. An opposite view would most likely be held by someone who pursues spiritual evolution.

It is from this perspective that we now consider Gurdjieff assertions about *the abnormal conditions of being-existence* established by Man.

To this end, we browsed through *The Tales* and extracted all the paragraphs containing this phrase. Then we grouped them together into related categories. We were then able to discuss these categories one-by-one.

## The Suggestibility of Man

Beelzebub introduces the factor of man's suggestibility early on in *The Tales* as he gradually familiarizes Hassein with mankind. Having first mentioned man's chief particularity – war – or, periodic outbreaks of reciprocal destruction, he says:

> "… *there are completely crystallized in them and there unfailingly become a part of their common presences–regardless of where they may arise and exist–functions which exist under the names 'egoism,' 'self-love,' 'vanity,' 'pride,' 'self-conceit,' 'credulity,' 'suggestibility,' and many other properties quite abnormal and quite unbecoming to the essence of any three-brained beings whatsoever.*

> "*Of these abnormal being-particularities, the particularity of their psyche the most terrible for them personally is that which is called 'suggestibility.'*[56]

He touches on the problem of suggestibility later in different contexts.

### *Suggestibility and Good Being-Customs*

Beelzebub points out that man's suggestibility is a result of the abnormal conditions of being-existence and is now a factor in the decline of good being customs. He says:

> "*The causes of the complete destruction and change of even this being-welfare for their tolerable existence achieved by time, both of good customs as well as 'moral usages,' are of course also engendered by these abnormal conditions for the ordinary being-existence around them established by them themselves.*

> "*As a concentrated result flowing from these abnormal conditions around them and which became the basic cause for this evil of theirs, there is a special property which arose not long ago in their psyche which they themselves call 'suggestibility.'*

Beelzebub mentions refers to this again, a little later, referring to suggestibility as a vice.

> "*After Germany, I had for a short time the place of my existence again there on the continent Europe among the beings of the com-*

---

[56] *The Tales, Ch XIV. The Beginnings of Perspectives Promising Nothing Very Cheerful, p107*

*munity called 'Italy'; and after Italy, among the beings of that com-
munity, who became for the beings of the community Russia what
are called the 'sources' for the satisfaction of that 'vice' which long
before had become fixed in the abnormal process of the ordinary
being-existence of terrestrial three-brained beings of recent centuries, and which is called 'suggestibility'; that is, I settled among the
beings of the community France.*

## Good Being-Customs

Elsewhere, Beelzebub comments on how good beings customs
combat evils that might otherwise arise because of the abnormally
established conditions of being-existence, saying:

*"And these customs are so deeply implanted in their everyday exis-
tence by their religion that at the present time, observing them me-
chanically without any wiseacring, beings are thereby more or less
ensured against several evils which, owing to the abnormally established conditions of being-existence, have been gradually formed
and still continue to be formed in uncountable numbers on that ill-
fated planet.*[57]

While suggestibility is undoubtedly a force in establishing good
being-customs, it also leads to their demise.

## Fashion

Beelzebub depicts fashion as a maleficent of suggestibility, with the
following words:

*"Adiat, Haidia, or fashions, are like our customs for daily being-ex-
istence which are established for the daily use of the three-brained
beings for the alleviation of inevitable exterior conditions independent of beings, and which usually gradually enter everywhere into
the daily use of beings as a necessary need, essential for them. These
said contemporary customs or fashions of theirs are, firstly, only
temporary and thus serve for the satisfaction only of the personal
insignificant aims of these present and future Hasnamusses, which
become phenomenally abnormal and trivially egoistic; and secondly, they are neither more nor less than the results of automatic
Reason based on that relative understanding, which generally flows*

---

[57] *The Tales, Ch XLII. Beelzebub in America, p977*

102

*from the abnormally established conditions there of ordinary be-
ing-existence.*[58]

When describing America and Americans, Beelzebub again mentions the topic of fashion, saying:

> *"The point is, that from the very beginning of this latest contempo-
> rary civilization of theirs, it somehow so fell out among the beings
> of all the innumerable separate groups there, that, of the seven as-
> pects of the fundamental commandment given to three-brained be-
> ings from Above, namely, 'strive to acquire inner and outer purity,'
> the single aspect they selected and in a distorted form have made
> their ideal, is that aspect which is conveyed in the following words:*

> *"'Help everything around you, both the animate and the still inan-
> imate, to acquire a beautiful appearance.'*

> *"And indeed, and especially in the last two centuries there, they
> have striven simply to attain a 'beautiful exterior' – but, of course,
> only in regard to those various objects external to them themselves,
> which chanced in the given period to become as they expressed it
> 'fashionable.'*

> *"During this said period, it has been of no concern to them whether
> any object external to them themselves had any substance whatso-
> ever – all that was necessary was that it should have what they call
> 'a striking appearance.'*[59]

## Suggestibility and the Lust for Gold

Beelzebub tells the tale of the Persian King who, believing that it
was possible to manufacture gold, assembled many of the learned
beings of Earth in Babylon in the hope of discovering the secret to
this process. The idea that this could be achieved was invented by
Harnahoom, whose essence later became crystallized into an 'Eter-
nal-Hasnamussian-individual.'

Beelzebub relates:

> *"In order to understand thoroughly which fundamental aspect en-
> suing from the total results of the abnormally established condi-
> tions of ordinary being-existence there gave rise to the said*

---

[58] *The Tales, Ch XXXVII. France, p689*
[59] *The Tales, Ch XLII. Beelzebub in America, p949*

*peculiarity of this Persian king, I must first enlighten you in respect of two facts which had become fixed long before.[60]*

The two facts are: that men become happy when they acquire a great deal of gold, and that kings who are victorious in war usually steal everything from the enemy they defeat (land, young women and accumulated "riches.") In this instance, however, the victorious Persian king simply stole the leaned beings from the countries he conquered because the idea that gold could be manufactured had been suggested to him.

## Suggestibility and Self-Calming

Beelzebub comments on Tolstoy's attempt to write his own version of *The Gospels[61]*, noting that while Tolstoy was reputed to be a great writer, he lacked any understanding of the human psyche. He notes that Tolstoy had "authority" because he was regarded as an accomplished writer.

The habit of repeating the opinion of "authorities" as their own is now a characteristic of man. Beelzebub says:

*"This strange trait of their general psyche, namely, of being satisfied with just what Smith or Brown says, without trying to know more, became rooted in them already long ago, and now they no longer strive at all to know anything cognizable by their own active deliberations alone.*

*"Concerning all this it must be said that neither the organ Kundabuffer which their ancestors had is to blame, nor its consequences which, owing to a mistake on the part of certain Sacred Individuals, were crystallized in their ancestors and later began to pass by heredity from generation to generation.*

*"But they themselves were personally to blame for it, and just on account of the abnormal conditions of external ordinary being-existence which they themselves have gradually established and which have gradually formed in their common presence just what has*

---

[60] *The Tales, Ch XXIV. Beelzebub's Flight to the Planet Earth for the Fifth Time, p323*

[61] *Leo Tolstoy's The Gospel in Brief is a combination the four Gospels into a single narrative of Jesus' life, into which Tolstoy merged his own religious ideas and beliefs. It led to his excommunication.*

*now become their inner 'Evil-God,' called 'Self-Calming.'*[62]

## Oskiano and Education

Gurdjieff is deeply critical of man's approach to education. The derivation of the word *Oskiano* indicates the importance Gurdjieff placed on effective education.

The ending *ano* (also *arno*) indicates a sacred process. The *ano* suffix relates to the Greek ανόδος (*anodos*) which means "the road up." *Oski* derives from the Armenian word *osk* for money, and means "gold." So *Oskiano* implies the process of making gold.

### The Nature of Human 'Education'

In discussing the disharmony of man's common presence, Beelzebub elaborates in considerable detail. He says:

> *"In order that you should better represent to yourself and understand the results flowing from such an astonishing 'psychic property,' you must first of all know about two facts actualized in the common presences of these favorites of yours.*
>
> *"One of these facts is produced in their common presence thanks to the existing cosmic law of 'self-adaption-of-Nature'; and the other fact flows from the abnormal conditions of ordinary being-existence established by them themselves about which I have repeatedly spoken.*
>
> *"The first fact is, that from the time when owing to their abnormal existence there began to be formed in them what is called the 'two-system-Zoostat,' that is, two independent consciousnesses, then Great Nature began gradually to adapt Herself and finally adapted Herself to this, that after they arrive at a certain age, there begin to proceed in them two 'Inkliazanikshanas' of different what are called 'tempos,' that is, as they themselves would say, two 'blood circulations' of different kind.*
>
> *"From this certain age mentioned, each one of these 'Inkliazanikshanas' of different tempo, that is to say each 'blood circulation,' begins to evoke in them the functioning of one of their*

---

mentioned consciousnesses; and vice versa, the intensive functioning of either consciousness begins to evoke in them the kind of blood circulation corresponding to it.

"The difference between these two independent kinds of blood circulation in their common presences is actualized by means of what is called 'tempo-Davlaksherian-circulation,' or, according to the expression there of what is called contemporary medicine, the 'difference-of-the-filling-of-the-blood-vessels'; that is to say, in the condition of the waking state, the 'center-of-gravity-of-the-blood-pressure' in their common presences obtains in one part of the general system of blood vessels, and in the condition of the passive state, in another part of the vessels.

"And the second fact – the fact ensuing from the abnormal conditions of the being-existence of your favorites – is that when, from the very beginning of the arising of their offspring, they intentionally try by every kind of means, for the purpose of making them respond to these abnormal conditions round them, to fix in their 'logicnestarian-localizations' as many impressions as possible obtained exclusively only from such artificial perceptions as are again due to the results of their abnormal existence – which maleficent action of theirs towards their offspring they call 'education' – then the totality of all such artificial perceptions gradually segregates itself in their common presences and acquires its own independent functioning, connected only as much with the functioning of their planetary body as is necessary merely for its automatic manifestation, and the totality of these artificial perceptions is then perceived by them, owing to their naiveté, as their real 'consciousness.' But as for the sacred data for genuine being-consciousness put into them by Great Nature – which consciousness ought to be possessed by them from the very beginning of their preparation for responsible existence together with the properties inherent in them which engender in them the genuine sacred being-impulses of 'faith,' 'hope,' 'love,' and 'conscience' – these data, becoming gradually also isolated and being left to themselves, evolve independently of the intentions of the responsible beings, and of course also independently of the bearers of them themselves, and come to be regarded as what is called the 'subconsciousness.'[63]

---

[63] *The Tales, Ch XXXII. Hypnotism, p565-566*

Several things are worth highlighting. Beelzebub points to the abnormal conditions of being-existence as being the cause of the arising of a dual being-consciousness. Great Nature was obliged to adapt herself accordingly.

Gurdjieff describes this need to adapt as a cosmic law, which he calls the *self-adaption-of-Nature*. We can think of this as having two aspects. First, for every cosmos there is a Trogoautoegocratic process that maintains the cosmos. In the case of Great Nature humanity is a part of this, and if humanity does not produce the substances Great Nature requires, then Great Nature must inevitably adapt. Secondly, Great Nature has responsibility both for feeding the Moon and also for transmitting the influences of the planets to the planet Earth. If, because of changes to the cosmos of humanity, these responsibilities cannot be met, then Great Nature will adapt.

The dual consciousness leads to men being hypnotizable - one technique for this being the manipulation of man's blood circulations.

Finally, man's education of children stems from the abnormal conditions of being-existence, and brings about this dual consciousness. Beelzebub repeats this assertion in a slightly different way in the following excerpt:

> "Their, in the objective sense, extreme misfortune about that which you yourself already 'perplexedly-instinctively suspect,' as I discern from the formulation of your question, especially from your having mentioned Oskiano, consists just in this, that they, having indeed at their arising such possibilities in themselves, immediately fall from the very first days after the separation from their mother's womb – only thanks to the abnormalities established in the process of ordinary being-existence of beings around them who have already reached responsible age – under the stubborn influence of that maleficent means, invented by them themselves for themselves, which as I already told you, represents in itself a something of the kind of Oskiano which they call 'education.'

> "And in consequence, in this way all possibilities for the free formation of all that which is required for the engendering of objective be-

*ing-Reason is gradually atrophied and finally disappears in these unfortunate, so to say, 'still-innocent-in-everything' newly arising beings during the period of their what is called 'preparatory age,' and as a result, when these newly arising beings later become responsible beings, they, in their, so to say, 'essence-center-of-gravity,' become the possessors, not of that objective-Reason which they ought to have, but of that strange totality of automatically perceived artificial even deceptive impressions which, having nothing in common with the localization of their spiritualized being-parts, nevertheless acquires a connection with the separate functionings of their common presence. In consequence of this, not only the whole process of their existence flows automatically, but also almost the whole process of the functioning of their planetary body becomes dependent only on chance, automatically perceived, external impressions.*[64]

The consequence of such education is that instead of the possibility of developing objective reason, the growing child will most likely live an automatized life.

## The Expression of Joy

In explaining the incident that provoked the sad suicide of two girls at a school in Russia, Beelzebub notes that they were capable of sincere happiness, as they had not yet been tainted by the abnormally established conditions of being-existence in that country. Their psyche had not yet become dual.

*"... picture to yourself that the sudden appearance of that quadruped animal called 'bull,' such as she had seen at home on the farm and which had enjoyed there the affection of all the children, who secretly even took it bread from the table, was to this as yet unformed impressionable young girl a shock for the corresponding associations under the influence of which, she, being full of a feeling of sincere happiness still unspoiled by the abnormally established conditions of being-existence, instantly wished to share her happiness with her bosom friend who was some distance off, and shouted to her to look at that dear bull.*[65]

---

[64] *The Tales, Ch XL. Beelzebub Tells How People Learned and Again Forgot about the Fundamental Cosmic Law of Heptaparaparshinokh, p815-816*
[65] *The Tales, Ch XLII. Beelzebub in America, p1040*

On Earth, the expression of sincere joy evaporates long before the age of responsibility is attained. It is worth noting here that the two girls in this story are named Mary (mother of Christ) and Elizabeth (mother of John The Baptist).

## Capitalist Education

When describing America, Beelzebub notes that America has become dependent on immigration from other continents of specialist professionals to support their ordinary existence. This may be literally true now in respect of some jobs in America that are carried out almost entirely immigrant labor. However the passage is best understood metaphorically. He says:

> "Among them there at the present time, these surrounding conditions of ordinary collective existence have already become such, that if, for some reason or other, the specialist professionals of all the kinds necessary for their ordinary collective existence should cease to come to them from the other continents to 'earn money,' then it is safe to say that within a month the whole established order of their ordinary existence would completely break down, since there would be none among them who could even so much as bake bread.

> "The chief cause of the gradual resulting of such an abnormality there among them is, on the one side, the law established by them themselves in respect of the rights of parents over their children and on the other hand the institution in schools for children of what is called a 'dollar savings bank' together with the principle of implanting in children a love of such dollars.[66]

As regards the literal meaning in this last paragraph, there is nothing particular about parental rights over children in the US that does not apply elsewhere. Parents have the right to make decisions about their children's upbringing, including their education, medical care, and religious upbringing. Parental rights were part of a body of law developed in England that was brought to the US by the early settlers.

Treating the same paragraph as allegory, we can regard the US as representing the modern personality, because it leads the world in

---

[66] *The Tales, Ch XLII. Beelzebub in America p922*

its economic, technological and social organization and in its ideas in these areas. The paragraph suggests that essence is smothered by a personality that is devoted to capitalism.

The development of capitalism has been a particular feature of US governance almost since its founding. Elsewhere, in *Paris Meetings 1943* for example, Gurdjieff's uses money as a metaphor for the energy of Being.

Thus to some degree, capitalism has been integrated into the abnormal conditions of being-existence.

## The Habit of Wiseacring

Gurdjieff frequently used the word "wiseacre" as a verb, meaning "to pretend to wisdom or knowledge, that you do not have." Wiseacring is thus a specific form of lying.

In *The Tales*, Beelzebub describes how wiseacring severely damaged the teachings of Saint Buddha. He remarks:

> "… to the grief of every Individual with Pure Reason of any gradation whatsoever and to the misfortune of the three-brained beings of all succeeding generations who arise on that planet, the first succeeding generation of the contemporaries of this genuine Messenger from Above, Saint Buddha, also began, owing once again to that same particularity of their psyche, namely, of wiseacring – which until now is one of the chief results of the conditions of the ordinary being-existence abnormally established there – to wiseacre with all His indications and counsels, and this time to 'super-wiseacre' so thoroughly that there reached the beings of the third and fourth generations nothing else but what our Honorable Mullah Nassr Eddin defines by the words:

> "'Only-information-about-its-specific-smell.'[67]

The habit of wiseacring, even with sacred teachings, became a facet of man's abnormal being-existence. Man's suggestibility turns wiseacring into an effective strategy for establishing power and influence.

---

[67] *The Tales, Ch XXI. The First Visit of Beelzebub to India, p239-240*

## The Desire to be "Learned"

The desire to be thought of as a "learned" man is described by Beelzebub as a "psycho-organic-need" of some men. In discussing how the law of Heptaparaparshinokh was once understood in China, even among common people, but how knowledge of it was eventually destroyed, Beelzebub explains:

*"To the regret of all more or less conscious 'relatively independent' separate Individuals of our Great Megalocosmos and to the misfortune of all subsequent three-brained beings who arose on this ill-fated planet of yours during the mentioned period, namely, during two to three of their centuries, the gradual distortion and ultimate almost total destruction began of just that blessing which had been created for them by their great ancestors thanks to their conscious labors and intentional sufferings.*

*"This followed from two causes.*

*"The first cause was, that thanks to the same abnormal conditions of external being-existence established by them themselves, certain of them were formed into responsible beings with that special 'organic-psychic-need' which in their speech might be formulated thus:*

*"'An-irresistible-thirst-to-be-considered-as-learned-by-beings-around-them-similar-to-themselves'; and such a 'psycho-organic-need' began to engender in them that strange inherency about which I have many times spoken and which is called by them 'cunning wiseacring.'*

*"By the way, my boy, bear in mind once for all that when I used and will use the expression 'learned beings of new formation' I referred and will refer to those of your favorites, the learned beings just mentioned by me, who have this specific inherency.*

*"The other cause was that thanks at that period to certain external circumstances not depending on them, and which ensue from common-cosmic processes, chiefly owing to the action of the law of Solioonensius, the being-data crystallized in them which engendered the impulses of what are called 'sensing' and 'foreseeing' began to weaken in the common presences of the genuine initiated beings and they began to take such newly formed types as I have just described and to initiate them into some of the totalities of the true information known to them alone, among which was also that*

*totality I mentioned, and from that time on this branch of genuine knowledge, which had already at that time become the possession of most of them, gradually began to be distorted and was ultimately again nearly quite forgotten.* [68]

The abnormal conditions of being-existence (established by them themselves) engendered an organic-psychic-need in some men to be considered learned. This need, it seems, was possessed a Chinese initiate named Chai-Yoo, who became a scientist of new formation. His cunning wiseacring, in his invention of a simplified new sound-producing instrument, based on some details of the Lav-Merz-Nokh, led to the current Western misunderstanding of the musical octave.

## Pecking to Death

Beelzebub highlights the "pecking to death" by learned beings of new formation, of other learned beings who, like Mesmer, possess genuine knowledge. The pecking to death is a common strategy in their efforts to establish their primacy over any competitive ideas or theories.

> *"Possibly now, in your presence also there already begin to be crystallized the data for the engendering always in corresponding cases of the being-impulse of an 'indubitable conviction' concerning this fact that thanks only to the learned beings of new formation there, in whom there has already been implanted the mentioned particularity, namely, of not failing to peck to death every colleague of theirs who does not do the same as has already been fixed by the abnormally established conditions of ordinary being-existence established there, there will never proceed in the presences of the three-brained beings of this ill-fated planet Earth of yours what is called the sacred 'Antkooano,' upon which, among other things, the Very Saintly Ashiata Shiemash also counted.*[69]

The unfortunate consequence here is that what is called the sacred 'Antkooano' does not occur on Earth. This process of perfecting Ob-

---

[68] *The Tales, Ch XL. Beelzebub Tells How People Learned and Again Forgot about the Fundamental Cosmic Law of Heptaparaparshinokh, p842*

[69] *The Tales, Ch XXXII. Hypnotism, p562-563*

jective-Reason in a three-brained being ought naturally to occur simply with the passage of time, but can only take place on planets where all cosmic truths are learned, shared and become known by everyone. Objective-Reason is then achieved through conscious labors and intentional suffering. The destructive activity of learned being of new formation eliminates this possibility.

## The Imagined Authority of Well-known Actors

As well as man's belief in the authority of so-called experts, in recent times undue respect is given to the opinions and proclamations of well-known actors. Speaking to Hassein about contemporary actors, Beelzebub offers specific advice on how to interact with such individuals. He explains as follows:

> "Every one of them really being in respect of genuine essence almost what is called a nonentity, that is, something utterly empty but enveloped in a certain visibility, they have gradually acquired such an opinion of themselves, by means of favorite exclamations always and everywhere repeated by them themselves like 'genius,' 'talent,' 'gift,' and still a number of other words empty also like themselves, that it is as if, among similar beings around them, only they have 'divine origin,' only they are almost 'God.'

> "Now listen and try to transubstantiate for use, at the proper time in the corresponding parts of your common presence, my really very practical advice.

> "This practical advice of mine is that, if for some reason or other you should have to exist, particularly in the near future, among the three-brained beings of that planet Earth which has taken your fancy – I say in the near future, because the presences of these three-brained beings who have taken your fancy and all the already fixed exterior conditions of their ordinary being-existence frequently degenerate – and if you should have some work or other there, proper to every conscious three-brained being, which has as its basis the aim of attaining welfare for surrounding beings, and the fulfillment of which depends partly on them themselves, then in whatever community of the contemporary civilization this may proceed, if you should have to meet in the interests of your work these contemporary terrestrial types in what are called their 'circles,' you must never

*fail to be very, very careful and take every kind of requisite measures to keep on good terms with them.*

*"Why you must be so careful towards just them, and in order that you may in general better represent to yourself and understand from every aspect these terrestrial contemporarily arisen types, I must without fail mention two further facts which became quite clear there.*

*"The first is that, owing as always to the same conditions of ordinary being-existence abnormally established there, and also to the existing 'illusorily inflated' maleficent idea of their famous art, these representatives of art gradually become crowned, as I have already said, with an imaginary halo in the preconceived picturings and notions of other three-brained beings there, and thereby automatically acquire an undeserved authority, in consequence of which all the rest of your favorites always and in everything assume that any opinion they express is authoritative and beyond dispute.[70]*

Because of the conditions of ordinary being-existence, men hold the opinions of well-known actors in high regard for no good reason. (In recent times, this has extended to include most celebrities.) Beelzebub advises Hassein to stay on the good side of such 'sensitive individuals' and flatter them for fear of arousing their enmity.

## The Degeneration of Man's Spiritual Life

As Beelzebub proceeds with his descriptions and explanations of the behavior of man, he makes clear that there was a "fall" that was triggered by the implanting and later removal of the organ Kundabuffer. He explains:

*"… in the beginning, after the organ Kundabuffer with all its properties had been removed from their presences, the duration of their existence was according to the 'Fulasnitamnian' principle, that is to say, they were obliged to exist until there was coated in them and completely perfected by reason what is called the 'body-Kesdjan,' or, as they themselves later began to name this being-part of theirs—of which, by the way, contemporary beings know only*

---

[70] *The Tales, Ch XXX. Art, p514-515*

*by hearsay—the 'Astral-body.'[71]*

Later, as men began to behave abnormally, and consequently ceased to emanate the vibrations required by Nature for the maintenance of the Moon and Anulios, Nature was compelled replace the Fulasnitamnian principle with the principle 'Itoklanoz.' This meant actualizing men according to the same principle that Nature applies to one-brained and two-brained beings.

Beelzebub says:

> *"And meanwhile remember, that although the fundamental motives for the diminution of the duration of the existence of the three-brained beings of this planet were from causes not depending on them, yet nevertheless, subsequently, the main grounds for all the sad results were – and particularly now continue to be – the abnormal conditions of external ordinary being-existence established by them themselves. Owing to these conditions the duration of their existence has, down to the present time, continued to become shorter and shorter, and now is already diminished to such a degree that, at the present time, the difference between the duration of the process of the existence of the three-brained beings of other planets in the whole of the Universe and the duration of the process of the existence of the three-brained beings of the planet Earth has become the same as the difference between the real duration of their existence and the duration of the existence of the infinitesimal beings in that drop of water we took as an example.[72]*

The reduction in the duration of life Beelzebub refers to here is its subjective duration in the sense of the experience of moments of presence. Two lives of equal duration in years may have very different subjective durations if one life contains many moments of presence and the other contains few.

Nevertheless, according to Beelzebub there has also been a general reduction in the length of life due to our abnormal conditions of existence. Thus this reduction in the duration of life also affected the Buddha himself, as Beelzebub notes here:

---

[71] *The Tales, Ch XVI. The Relative Understanding of Time, p131*
[72] *The Tales, Ch XVI. The Relative Understanding of Time, p131*

*"'But in consequence of the fact that before the period of the said Sacred Individual's appearance here, the duration of your existence had, owing to very many firmly fixed abnormal conditions of ordinary existence created by yourselves, already become abnormally short, and therefore the process of sacred Rascooarno had also very soon to occur to this Sacred Individual, that is to say, he also had, like you, to die prematurely, then after his death, the former conditions were gradually re-established there owing on the one hand to the established abnormal conditions of ordinary being-existence and, on the other hand, to that maleficent particularity in your psyche, called Wiseacring.*[73]*

He returns to this topic later in the book. While observing Earth from Mars, Beelzebub notices that man's life span is diminishing. He notes:

*"Of course when I first noticed this, I at once took into account not only the chief particularity of their psyche, that is their periodic reciprocal destruction, but also the innumerable what are called 'illnesses' which exist exclusively only on that planet, the majority of which, by the way, arose and continue to arise owing to the same abnormal external conditions of the ordinary being-existence established by them, which help to make it impossible for them to exist normally up to the sacred Rascooarno.*[74]*

## The Formation of Man's Subconscious

Because of the principle Itoklanoz man's essence has less possibility of development. Beelzebub notes that most of the causes of the strangeness of their psyche are to be found in man's essence. He explains:

*"Just at the beginning of this sixth personal sojourn of mine I soon categorically made clear, thanks to my experimental investigations, that most of the causes of the strangeness of their psyche are found not in that usual consciousness of theirs, in which alone they have already automatized themselves to exist in what is called their waking state, but in that consciousness of theirs which, thanks to their abnormal ordinary being-existence, was gradually driven within*

---

[73] *The Tales, Ch XXIII. The Fourth Personal Soiourn of Beelzebub on the Planet Earth, p283*
[74] *The Tales, Ch XXIV. Beelzebub's Flight to the Planet Earth for the Fifth Time, p319*

*their common presence and which although it should have been their real consciousness, yet remains in them in its primitive state and is called their 'subconsciousness.'*[75]

## Our Buried Conscience

An important consequence of this burying of essence, is that man's true conscience was buried with it. The Legominism of the Very Saintly Ashiata Shiemash, titled "The Terror-of-the-Situation," describes this: Ashiata wrote:

> *"'During the period of my year of special observations on all of their manifestations and perceptions, I made it categorically clear to myself that although the factors for engendering in their presences the sacred being-impulses of Faith, Hope, and Love are already quite degenerated in the beings of this planet, nevertheless, the factor which ought to engender that being-impulse on which the whole psyche of beings of a three-brained system is in general based, and which impulse exists under the name of Objective-Conscience, is not yet atrophied in them, but remains in their presences almost in its primordial state.*
>
> *"'Thanks to the abnormally established conditions of external ordinary being-existence existing here, this factor has gradually penetrated and become embedded in that consciousness which is here called "subconsciousness," in consequence of which it takes no part whatever in the functioning of their ordinary consciousness.*[76]

Man's abnormal conditions of being-existence have served to bury his Objective Conscience – an important facet of man's nature that Ashiata chooses to exploit, and which presents a possibility for contemporary man.

## Ashiata's Circumvention

In organizing for the spread of his teaching, Ashiata Shiemash established relations with the brotherhood 'Tchaftantouri' which was situated not far from Djoolfapal. Beelzebub recounts:

---

[75] *The Tales, Ch XXXI. The Sixth and Last Sojourn of Beelzebub on the Planet Earth, p530*
[76] *The Tales, Ch XXVI. The Legominism Concerning the Deliberations of the Very Saintly Ashiata Shiemash under the Title of "The Terror-of-the-Situation.", p359*

*"And so, after arriving in the town Djoolfapal, the Very Saintly Ashiata Shiemash established corresponding relations with these brethren of the mentioned brotherhood who were working upon that abnormally proceeding functioning of their psyche which they themselves had constated, and he began enlightening their Reason by means of objectively true information, and guiding their being-impulses in such a way that they could sense these truths without the participation either of the abnormally crystallized factors already within their presences, or of the factors which might newly arise from the results of the external perceptions they obtained from the abnormally established form of ordinary being-existence.[77]*

Man's abnormally established form of being-existence serves as a barrier to receiving objectively true information, which Ashiata takes steps to circumvent.

## The Tibetan Isolation

Emphasizing the importance to Man of isolating himself from the abnormal conditions of being-existence, as Ashiata did for his pupils. Beelzebub mentions the beneficent effect of such isolation in the chapter on Religion.[78]

He points out that because of Tibet's isolation, Tibetans had (until recently) been little affected by abnormally established conditions of ordinary being-existence on the Earth.

*"Now, as regards the fifth teaching, namely, the teaching of Saint Lama, also a genuine messenger from our ENDLESSNESS, the teaching of this Sacred Individual was spread among those three-brained beings there, who, on account of the geographical conditions, scarcely ever happened to come into contact with other beings of this ill-starred planet, and in consequence have scarcely been affected by the abnormally established conditions of ordinary being-existence there.[79]*

---

[77] *The Tales, Ch XXVII. The Organization for Man's Existence Created by the Very Saintly Ashiata Shiemash, p368*

[78] *The Tales, Ch XXXVIII. Religion, p694*

[79] *The Tales, Ch XXXVIII. Religion, p705*

## The Difficulty of Self-perfection

Nevertheless, the general outcome of the abnormal conditions of being-existence, for man, is that self-perfection is far more difficult than it might otherwise be. Beelzebub explains that at a three-brained being's arising, when the process of Djartklom happens in the Omnipresent-Okidanokh, the three holy forces of the sacred Triamazikamno are deposited in the being.

As a direct consequence they can perfect themselves by utilizing these forces by consciously and intentionally fulfilling their being-Partkdolg-duty. Thus they can become individuals who have their own sacred law of Triamazikamno.

This helps them take in and use all that is holy in their common presence, aiding the functioning of Objective or Divine Reason in them.

But ...

> "But the great terror of it, my boy, lies just in this, that although in those three-brained beings who have interested you and who breed on the planet Earth, there arise and are present in them, up to the time of their complete destruction, these three independent localizations or three being-brains, through which separately all the three holy forces of the sacred Triamazikamno which they might also utilize for their own self-perfecting are transformed and go for further corresponding actualizations, yet, chiefly on account of the irregular conditions of ordinary being-existence established by them themselves, these possibilities beat their wings in vain.[80]

The difficulty arises because man's ordinary being-existence does not encourage fulfilling being-Partkdolg-duty. In fact, a few pages later Beelzebub remarks that men have entirely ceased to fulfill being-Partkdolg-duty:

> "And so, my boy, the process of Djartklom in the Omnipresent-Okidanokh proceeds in the presence of each of these favorites of yours, and in them also, all its three holy forces are blended independently with other cosmic crystallizations, and go for the corre-

---

[80] *The Tales, Ch XVII. The Arch-Absurd: According to the Assertion of Beelzebub, Our Sun Neither Lights nor Heats, p145*

*sponding actualizations, but as, chiefly owing to the already mentioned abnormal conditions of being-existence gradually established by them themselves, they have entirely ceased to fulfill being-Partkdolg-duty, then, in consequence of this, none of those holy sources of everything existing, with the exception of the denying source alone, is transubstantiated for their own presences.*[81]

One consequence of this is that almost all of these three-brained beings only possess automatic-Reason. Beelzebub explains:

*"It seems to me I already once told you that although from the period you mentioned on that planet almost all the three-brained beings there became, thanks to the abnormally established conditions of ordinary being-existence, possessors of only an automatic-Reason, nevertheless it does sometimes happen there that certain of them by chance escape this common fate and that instead of that automatic-Reason which has become usual there, a genuine objective 'being-Reason' is formed in certain of them as it is in all three-centered beings of our great Megalocosmos.*

*"Although such exceptions, especially during recent centuries, are very rare there, yet, I repeat, they nevertheless do occur.*[82]

In summary, man's reason has degenerated to the point where it is entirely automatic reasoning.

## The Loss of Allegorical Transmission

Beelzebub points out that because of man's deterioration in being mentation, the transmission of ideas and knowledge by allegorical means has ceased. He mentions this in relation to contemporary man's ability to ponder the meanings of The Gospels. He notes:

*"They do not consider that at that period 'being-mentation' among the beings of this planet was still nearer to that normal mentation, which in general is proper to be present among three-brained beings, and that at that time the transmission of ideas and thoughts was in consequence still what is called 'Podobnisirnian,' or, as it is still otherwise said 'allegorical.'*

---

[81] *The Tales, Ch XVII. The Arch-Absurd: According to the Assertion of Beelzebub, Our Sun Neither Lights nor Heats, p147*

[82] *The Tales, Ch XL. Beelzebub Tells How People Learned and Again Forgot about the Fundamental Cosmic Law of Heptaparaparshinokh, p814*

*"In other words, in order to explain to themselves, or to any others, some act or other, the three-brained beings of the planet Earth then referred to the understanding of similar acts which had already formerly occurred among them.*

*"But, meanwhile, this also now proceeds in them according to the principle called 'Chainonizironness.'*

*"And this first proceeded there because, thanks as always to the same abnormally established conditions of ordinary existence, their being-mentation began to proceed without any participation of the functioning of their what are called 'localizations of feeling,' or according to their terminology 'feeling center,' chiefly in consequence of which this mentation of theirs finally became automatized.*[83]

So, man's mentation became automatized. However Nature needed to adapt. As Beelzebub explains, it was necessary, despite man's automatized life, for men to produce some higher substances – in order to provide some nourishment to higher centers.

*"Unfortunately Nature there was compelled to adapt herself to this abnormality, so that, owing to these unexpectednesses, certain intense being-experiencings and active deliberations might proceed in them automatically, independently of them themselves and so that, owing to these 'active deliberations,' the required transformation and assimilation of these necessary sacred particles of the higher being-foods might automatically proceed in them.*[84]

So, Nature organized the production of a small amount of higher substances to occur automatically.

### The Inaccurate Historical Record

In addition to the loss by Man of the ability to ponder sacred text from an allegorical perspective, there is the considerable difficulty of passing any true information from generation to generation. After using the expression the 'Building-of-the-Tower-of-Babel,' and noting that this expression is often used by the contemporary three-brained beings of Earth, Beelzebub says:

*"I wish to touch upon this expression frequently used there and to*

---

[83] *The Tales, Ch XXXVIII. Religion, p738*
[84] *The Tales, Ch XXXIX. The Holy Planet "Purgatory", p784*

*elucidate it to you chiefly because firstly I chanced to be a witness at that time of all the events which gave rise to it, and secondly because the history of the arising of this expression and its transubstantiation in the understanding of your contemporary favorites can very clearly and instructively elucidate to you that, thanks as always to the same abnormally established conditions of ordinary being-existence, no precise information of events there which have indeed occurred to beings of former epochs ever reaches beings of later generations.*

*And if, by chance, something like this expression does reach them, then the fantastic Reason of your favorites constructs a whole theory on the basis of just one expression such as this, with the result that those illusory 'being-egoplastikoori,' or what they call 'psychic-picturings' increase and multiply in their presences owing to which there has arisen in the Universe the strange 'unique-psyche' of three-brained beings which every one of your favorites has.*[85]

The abnormal conditions of being-existence prevents the passing of accurate information down the generations and the tendency to wiseacre leads to contemporary men having inaccurate "psychic picturings" with which in turn leads Man to form an inaccurate world view.

## The Distortion of Our World View

Beelzebub also comments on man's world view, when discussing man's understanding of Justice and the fantastic idea of external Good and Evil:

*"The fundamental evil, for all these unfortunates, from this fantastic idea resulted there chiefly because, even before this – of course thanks always to the same conditions of ordinary being-existence established by them themselves – data ceased to be crystallized in them for the engendering of what is called 'various being-aspects of a world view,' and instead of this a 'world view' is formed in them based exclusively on that maleficent idea about external Good and Evil.*[86]

---

[85] *The Tales, Ch XXIV. Beelzebub's Flight to the Planet Earth for the Fifth Time, p331*
[86] *The Tales, Ch XLIV. In the Opinion of Beelzebub, Man's Understanding of Justice is for him in the Objective Sense an Accursed Mirage, p1141*

This incorrect idea of external Good and Evil has historically dominated man's world view and continues to do so. It is something that is never questioned, although it is a wrong idea.

## The Specific Degeneration of Man

The abnormal conditions of being-existence have, according to Beelzebub, caused specific disabilities in humanity.

### The Disease of Tomorrow

While relating Ashiata Shiemash's legominism, "The Terror-of-the-Situation," Beelzebub mentions the degeneration of "hope" in man. He says that, on a marble tablet in the possession of the Brotherhood-Olbogmek, is written a saying of Ashiata Shiemash which reads:

*'Faith,' 'Love', and 'Hope'*

*Faith of consciousness is freedom*
*Faith of feeling is weakness*
*Faith of body is stupidity.*

*Love of consciousness evokes the same in response*
*Love of feeling evokes the opposite*
*Love of body depends only on type and polarity.*

*Hope of consciousness is strength*
*Hope of feeling is slavery*
*Hope of body is disease.* [87]

Beelzebub comments on hope in Man with the following words:

*"And the personal observations and investigations I later specially made, regarding this said strange impulse present in them, clearly showed me that in truth the factors for engendering this abnormal impulse in their presences are most maleficent for them themselves.*

*"Thanks to this abnormal hope of theirs a very singular and most*

---

[87] *The Tales, Ch XXVI. The Tales, Ch XXVI. The Legominism Concerning the Deliberations of the Very Saintly Ashiata Shiemash under the Title of "The Terror-of-the-Situation.", p361*

*strange disease, with a property of evolving, arose and exists among them there even until now – a disease called there 'tomorrow.'*[88]

So, as the saying of Asiata Shiemash declares *"hope of feeling is slavery* and *hope of body is disease."* One of the consequences of this is the disease of tomorrow.

## Man's Ability to Vocalize

Beelzebub asserts that because of the conditions of ordinary being-existence every kind of human capability has deteriorated over time, including our ability to vocalize different sounds and use them in our languages. He describes this as follows:

> *"But later on, when thanks as always to the same conditions of ordinary being-existence abnormally established by themselves, every kind of property proper to the presences of three-brained beings gradually deteriorated, this 'being-ableness' also deteriorated in them and at such a tempo that whereas the beings of the Babylonian period could use for conversation among themselves only seventy-seven definite consonants, the deterioration continued at such a tempo after the Babylonian period, that five centuries later, the beings there could use at most only thirty-six definite 'letters,' and the beings of certain communities could not reproduce even this number of separate articulate sounds.*[89]

It is may be that this reduction in our vocal range limits our ability to express ourselves in some way, but if so this is never said. This was, incidentally, a limitation that even Gurdjieff himself suffered from - he was unable to pronounce the English "h" as in words like "have" and "hold." He substituted a "kh" into such words referring, for example, to Jane Heap as "Miss Kheap."

## Degeneration of Man's Sight

Beelzebub also mentions a deterioration in man's sight. In discussing the Teskooano constructed by the Akhaldans who survived the sinking of Atlantis and eventually settled in Egypt, Beelzebub ex-

---

[88] *The Tales, Ch XXVI. The Tales, Ch XXVI. The Legominism Concerning the Deliberations of the Very Saintly Ashiata Shiemash under the Title of "The Terror-of-the-Situation.", p362*
[89] *The Tales, Ch XXX. Art, p496*

plains how, when the three-brained beings of Earth were existing normally...

> ... they had what is called 'Olooestesnokhnian sight, they could also perceive, at a distance proper to be perceived by ordinary three-brained beings, the visibility of all great as well as small cosmic concentrations existing beyond them during every process of the Omnipresent-Okidanokh which proceeded in their atmosphere.

> "In addition, those of them who were consciously perfected and had thereby brought the sensibility of the perception of their organ of sight - like three-brained beings everywhere else - up to what is called the 'Olooessultratesnokhnian state,' acquired the possibility of perceiving also the visibility of all these cosmic units situated at the same distance, which arise and have their further existence dependent upon the crystallizations localized directly from the sacred Theomertmalogos, that is to say, from the emanations of our most holy Sun Absolute.

> "And later, when the same constant abnormal conditions of ordinary being-existence were finally established, as a consequence of which Great Nature was compelled, for reasons of which I have already once told you, among other limitations, also to degenerate the functioning of their organ of sight into what is called 'Koritesnokhnian,' that is to say, into the sight proper to the presences of one-brained and two-brained beings, then thereafter they were able to perceive the visibility of their great as well as their small concentrations situated beyond them only when the sacred process 'Aieioiuoa' proceeded in the Omnipresent Active Element Okidanokh in the atmosphere of their planet, or, as they themselves say – according to their understanding and their own perceptions – 'on dark nights.'[90]

Here Beelzebub is describing the degeneration of Man's sight as being a consequence of Great Nature having to alter Man's functioning from Fulasnitamnian to Itoklanoz. The organ of sight that Beelzebub refers to here is almost certainly not the eyes.

---

[90] *The Tales, Ch XXIII. The Fourth Personal Sojourn of Beelzebub on the Planet Earth, p305*

## Failing To See One's Own Defects

Beelzebub recommends to Hassein that when he wishes to get on the "good side" of any man or woman, he should make a habit of asking their advice, because of their "psycho-organic-need" to "teach others sense." Speaking of this need, he explains:

> "This special property formed in their psyche, thanks of course also always to the same abnormally established conditions of ordinary being-existence, becomes as it were – when each one of them already becomes a responsible being – an obligatory part of his presence.
>
> "Everyone there without exception has this 'psycho-organic need'; old and young, men and women and even those whom they call 'prematurely born.'
>
> "The mentioned 'particular need' of theirs arises in them, in its turn, thanks to another particular property of theirs which is that from the very moment when each of them acquires the capacity of distinguishing between 'wet' and 'dry,' then, carried away by this attainment, he ceases forever to see and observe his own abnormalities and defects, but sees and observes those same abnormalities and defects in others.[91]

## Cowardice

Beelzebub describes human cowardice from an unusual perspective when he points out the fear that many one and two-brained beings have for men. He says:

> "Although these being-data are still formed in the presences of certain terrestrial one-brained and two-brained beings of other exterior forms, as for example those named by them 'tigers,' 'lions,' 'bears,' 'hyenas,' 'snakes,' 'phalangas,' 'scorpions,' and so on, who have not had and do not now have in their mode of existence any contact or relation with these biped favorites of yours, nevertheless there is already formed in their common presences, thanks of course to the abnormally established conditions of the ordinary existence of your favorites, one very strange and highly interesting particularity, namely, that the enumerated beings, tigers, lions, bears, hyenas, snakes, phalangas, scorpions, and so on, perceive the inner feeling of

---

[91] *The Tales*, Ch XLIII. *Beelzebub's Survey of the Process of the Periodic Reciprocal Destruction of Men, or Beelzebub's Opinion of War*, p1075

*fear in other beings before them as enmity towards themselves, and therefore strive to destroy these others in order to avert the 'menace' from themselves.*

*"And this so happened because your favorites, thanks always to the same abnormal conditions of existence, have gradually become, as they themselves say, 'cowardly' from head to foot, and because at the same time the need of destroying the existence of others has been in-culcated in them, also from head to foot. And so, when they, being already cowards 'of the highest degree,' are about to destroy the ex-istence of the beings of these other forms, or when they chance to meet such beings – who it must be said, to their misfortune and to our regret, have become at the present time already much stronger than they, physically as well as in other being-attainments – then they become 'afraid,' as they say there in such case, 'to the point of wetness.'*[92]

He thus characterizes the destruction of other species (other be-ings) that men fear as cowardice. Both this cowardice, and also the fear that such species have of man, are consequences of man's abnor-mal conditions of being-existence.

## *The Disharmony Between Bobbin-Kandelnosts*

Explaining the deaths by thirds that he has witnessed – that is the death of one or another man's three brains prior to his his actual death, Beelzebub says:

*"Such deaths by thirds, there on the planet Earth which has taken your fancy, have occurred particularly frequently during the last two centuries, and they occur to those of your favorites who, thanks either to their profession, or to one of their what are called 'pas-sions,' arising and acquired by the beings belonging to all large and small communities there, on account of the same abnormally ar-ranged conditions of their ordinary being-existence, have during their being-existence lived through in a greater or smaller degree the contents of the Bobbin-kandelnost of one or another of their being-brains.*[93]

---

[92] *The Tales, Ch XLI. The Bokharian Dervish Hadji-Asvatz-Troov, p877*

[93] *The Tales, Ch XXIX. The Fruits of Former Civilizations and the Blossoms of the Contemporary, p442-443*

Beelzebub identifies the abnormally arranged conditions of man's ordinary being-existence as the cause of this. He subsequently identifies that Man could regulate the use of his centers to prevent such deaths by thirds, as there is a mechanism similar to the regulator on a watch that he could use to that end. He then laments...

> *"But even if they should understand such a simple secret it will be all just the same; they still would not make the necessary being-effort, quite accessible even to the contemporary beings and thanks to which, by the foresight of Nature, beings in general acquire the possibility of what is called 'harmonious association,' by virtue of which alone energy is created for active being-existence in the presence of every three-brained being and consequently in them themselves. But at the present time, this energy can be elaborated in the presences of your favorites only during their quite unconscious state, that is to say during what they call 'sleep.'*

> *"But in your favorites, specially in your contemporary favorites, who exist constantly passively under the direction of only one of the separate spiritualized parts of their common presence and thereby constantly manifest themselves entirely by their factors for negative properties also lawfully arisen in them, and hence, by negative manifestations, there proceeds in them that same disproportionate expenditure of the contents of their various Bobbin-kandelnosts, that is to say, the possibilities, placed in them by Nature according to law, of action by only one or only two of their brains, are always experienced, in consequence of which the contents of one or two of their Bobbin-kandelnosts are prematurely exhausted; whereupon, just like those mechanical watches in which the winding is run down or the force of their regulators is weakened, they cease to act.*[94]

### The Degeneration of Human Art

At the beginning of the *Chapter XXIX*, Ahoon suggests to Beelzebub that he should consider describing to Hassein what three-brained beings on Earth refer to as art, Beelzebub replies:

> *"Thank you, old man, for reminding me of this. It is true that I have scarcely even mentioned that indeed harmful factor – created also*

---

[94] *The Tales, Ch XXIX. The Fruits of Former Civilizations and the Blossoms of the Contemporary,* p445-446

*by them themselves – for the final atrophy even of those data for their being-mentation which by chance have still survived.*

Even though art has its origins in the efforts made by Babylonian learned beings to preserve knowledge so that it could be passed down to future generations, Beelzebub depicts its current manifestation as a harmful influence created by humanity itself.

## The Governance of Man

Through the words of Beelzebub, Gurdjieff declares war to be the chief particularity of mankind. It is not an outlandish assertion.

There has been no year since 1000 BCE when there have been no wars in the world. Even in the years of relative peace, the eras referred to as Pax Romana (27 BCE to 180 CE) and Pax Mongolica (1206CE to 1368 CE), which were periods of peace and prosperity in those empires, there were wars raging elsewhere on the globe.

If we are to believe historians then the causes of war are usually attributed to:

- **Imperial Ambition.** Sometimes ambitious leaders (Alexander The Great offers a good example) conduct a campaign of conquest in an effort to establish a large empire. Where such campaigns are successful they are paid for by the conquered.

- **Nationalism.** Nationalism can be geographic or tribal. Either way a sense of identification with a "nation," coupled with a belief in its "superiority" leads to revolutionary or international war.

- **Ideology.** Systems of beliefs and values, whether religious or simply economic can be deemed to be causes of war.

- **Geopolitics.** Sometimes the geography of borderlands between countries are cited as underlying causes of conflict.

- **Economic factors.** Economic decline and resource scarcity are sometimes thought to be the cause of civil or international wars.

- **Militarism:** The build up of military capability is sometimes regarded as a precursor to war. Once a country establishes a powerful military capability it is tempted to employ it.

## Solioonensius

Beelzebub discards all of these justifications and explanations for war, asserting that, no matter what the context, there is  a single cause. Commenting on the process of reciprocal destruction during the Bolshevik revolution in Russia, Beelzebub says:

> *"You remember I promised to relate to you about the fundamental real causes of this arch-phenomenal process.*
>
> *"Well, it is necessary to tell you that this grievous phenomenon arises there thanks to two independent factors, the first of which is the cosmic law Solioonensius, and the second is always the same abnormal conditions of ordinary being-existence established by them themselves.*
>
> *"In order that you should the better understand about both these factors, I will explain to you about each of them separately, and will begin by the cosmic law Solioonensius.*
>
> *"First of all you must be told that all the three-brained beings, on whatever planet they may arise, and whatever exterior coating they may receive, always await the manifestations of the action of this law with impatience and with joy, somewhat how your favorites await what are called their feasts of 'Easter,' 'Bairam,' 'Zadik,' 'Ramadan,' 'Kaialana,' and so on.*[95]

He makes the point that the impact of the cosmic law Solioonensius on man can be very beneficial, but because of the abnormal conditions of ordinary being-existence it can lead to bouts of reciprocal destruction. He notes that man's 'evil-inner-god' (self-calming) is implicated in this.

> *"But later, among the number of chief evils which flow from the conditions of ordinary being-existence established by them themselves, specially when in the presences of every terrestrial three-brained being, there began to become predominant the 'evil-inner-God' of theirs I mentioned, named there self-calming, then it oc-*

---

[95] *The Tales, Ch XXXIV. Russia, p622*

curred that in them under the influence of the action of Solioonen-sius, instead of the desire and striving for a speedier self-perfection a something began to arise such as they themselves characterize by the words 'need of freedom,' which chiefly serves the cause of the arising there of these same grievous processes of theirs similar to this last 'Bolshevism.'

"I will explain to you somewhat later how they represent to themselves this famous freedom of theirs, and now I will only tell you that that feeling which arises from the action of Solioonensius strengthens in them the need for some or other general change in the conditions of their ordinary external being-existence which until then were more or less stable.[96]

He subsequently notes that such revolutions don't improve man's life in those areas where they occur.

"These processes of theirs, if they had even but a little improved the existence of beings of subsequent generations, then perhaps, from the point of view of a strictly impartial observer, they might even not have appeared to be so terrifying, yet to the misfortune of all three-brained beings of our Great Universe, the calamity is just in this that as soon as the 'blissful action' of this cosmic lawful manifestation ceases, and these terrifying processes come to an end, then there again begins the old story and their ordinary being-existence becomes 'more bitter' than before, and, parallel with this, there also deteriorates what is called their 'sane-awareness-of-the-sense-and-aim-of- their-existence.'[97]

And ultimately it cannot be said that any of those involved in these terrifying processes are actually the cause. Such revolutions are simply enabled by the abnormal conditions of ordinary being-existence.

"They, as I have already said, could not even approximately consider and understand that, during these common planetary terrifying processes, individual persons are in no way the cause, and only by chance happen to be in those posts, the occupation of which, on account of the conditions of mutual existence which had already been established, compels them to manifest themselves in one or other role, the results of which roles, according to law-conformity

---

[96] *The Tales, Ch XXXIV. Russia, p623*
[97] *The Tales, Ch XXXIV. Russia, p628*

*entirely independent of them themselves, are cast into these or other forms.*[98]

## The Invention of the Means of Reciprocal Destruction

Irrespective of the cause of war, mankind perennially pursues the invention of the weaponry to prosecute it. When describing Gornahoor Harharkh's experiment to demonstrate the transformation of a fragment of red copper into intraplanetary metals of lower or higher degrees of vivifyingness, Beelzebub draws a parallel with the murderous behavior of men. He remarks:

> *"A rough parallel can be drawn between the occasional proceedings on your planet and the proceedings then in that small fragment of copper, if you imagine yourself high up and looking down upon a large public square, where thousands of your favorites, seized with the most intense form of their chief psychosis, are destroying each other's existence by all kinds of means invented by them themselves, and that in their places there immediately appear what are called their 'corpses,' which owing to the outrages done to them by the beings who are not yet destroyed, change color very perceptibly, as a result of which the general visibility of the surface of the said large square is gradually changed.*[99]

Beelzebub later mentions the direct German invention of weapons based on poison gas.

> *"About this German invention, I once also learned there among other things, that when one of the beings of that community, for reasons I recently described, happened to obtain this gas from some 'surplanetary' and 'intraplanetary' definite formations, and noticed in the said way its particularity, and told several others about it, then, owing to the fact that there was then proceeding in the presences of the beings of their community, consequently in them themselves, what is called 'the-most-intense-experiencing' of the chief particularity of the psyche of the three-brained beings of your planet, namely, 'the-urgent-need-to-destroy-the-existence-of-others-like-themselves' – and indeed, the beings of that community were then fully absorbed in their process of reciprocal destruction with*

---

[98] *The Tales, Ch XXXIV. Russia, p638*
[99] *The Tales, Ch XVIII. The Arch-preposterous, p174*

*the beings of neighboring communities – these others thereupon at once 'enthusiastically' decided to devote themselves entirely to finding means to employ the special property of that gas for the speedy mass destruction of the existence of the beings of other communities.*[100]

## State Organizations and the Division Into Castes

In discussing the saintly activities of Ashiata Shiemash Beelzebub notes that, within ten years, he witnessed the disappearance of two different "abnormally established conditions of being-existence':

> *"The total result, however, of everything I have mentioned, was that within ten terrestrial years there had disappeared of their own accord those two chief forms of ordinary being-existence abnormally established there, from which there chiefly flow and still continue to flow, most of the maleficent causes the totality of which engenders all kinds of trifling factors which prevent the establishment of conditions there for at least a normal outer being-existence for these unfortunate favorites of yours.* [101]

The two chief forms are the state organizations that Man creates and the assigning of people into different castes.

## Exploitation of Men by Men

In conformity with the above factors, the absence of objective conscience in Man has the consequence that the "prosperity of one is built on the adversity of many," as Beelzebub explains.

> *"Meanwhile transubstantiate in yourself the following: when the mentioned particular psychic property of 'egoism' had been completely formed in the common presences of these favorites of yours, and, later, there had also been formed in them various other secondary impulses already mentioned by me which ensued and now still continue to ensue from it – and furthermore, in consequence of the total absence of the participation of the impulse of sacred con-*

---

[100] *The Tales, Ch XXIX. The Fruits of Former Civilizations and the Blossoms of the Contemporary, p427*
[101] *The Tales, Ch XXVII. The Organization for Man's Existence Created by the Very Saintly Ashiata Shiemash, p375*

*science in their waking-consciousness – then these three-brained be-*
*ings arising and existing on the planet Earth, both before the period*
*of the Very Saintly Activities of Ashiata Shiemash and also since*
*have always striven and still continue to strive to arrange their wel-*
*fare during the process of their ordinary existence, exclusively for*
*them themselves.*

*"And as in general, on none of the planets of our great Universe*
*does there or can there exist enough of everything required for ev-*
*erybody's equal external welfare, irrespective of what are called 'ob-*
*jective-merits,' the result there is that the prosperity of one is always*
*built on the adversity of many.*[102]

Despite the political idealism that bubbles up at times in mankind
across the ages, the economic problem of "how to share scarce re-
sources between the many," always leads to a situation where wealth
is concentrated in the hands of the few.

## Corrupt or Unnecessary Bureaucracy

Describing the efforts he made to acquire a permit for operating a
laboratory in Moscow, Beelzebub notes.

*"I, however, on account of the short time I had stayed there, had*
*not yet had time to make clear for myself all the subtleties of the or-*
*dinary being-existence which had begun in this community, as I*
*said, to become particularly abnormal.*

*"That is why, when I set out to take steps to get the permit I re-*
*quired, there began for me those endless vexations, or, as they them-*
*selves say in such cases, the 'idiotic dilly-dallyings' which were also*
*fixed not long before in the process of their being-existence, and in*
*addition all this turned out in the end to be quite without result and*
*unnecessary.*[103]

Bureaucracy is not an inevitable feature of human state organization, but it is a common one. Here, as in other parts of *The Tales*
where state organization is discussed, the text can also be inter-

---

[102] *The Tales, Ch XXVII. The Organization for Man's Existence Created by the Very Saintly*
*Ashiata Shiemash, p383*
[103] *The Tales, Ch XXXIV. Russia, p606*

preted allegorical. The many 'I's are organized in a haphazard one-as-sociation-leading to-another manner.

## A Triumph of Self-Importance

Describing various attempts by Man to establish effective societies to eliminate the scourge of war, Beelzebub relates that none have been successful. He points to the cause; beings with Objective Reason never participate in such societies. He explains:

> *"The point is that in order to participate in any society whatsoever, a being must always of necessity be important and such a being there among them, thanks once again to the abnormally established conditions of being-existence, can only be one who either has a great deal of money or who becomes what is called 'famous' among the other beings there.*
>
> *"And since especially during recent times only those beings can become famous and important among them in whom the mentioned sacred function, namely 'being-conscience,' is entirely absent, then in consequence of the fact that this sacred function in the presences of beings is in general always associated with everything that represents and is Objective Reason, then, of course, those three-brained beings with Objective Reason always have conscience as well, and consequently such a being with conscience, will never be 'important' among the other beings.*[104]

## Inability to Think Sincerely

Hassein asks Beelzebub how it is that humanity is not aware of the horror of the reciprocal destruction they so frequently engage in. Beelzebub responds:

> *"A number of them do ponder even very often and, in spite of the automaticity of their Reason, they fully understand that this particularity of theirs, namely, their predisposition to periodic reciprocal destruction, is such an unimaginable horror and such a hideousness that no name can even be found for it.*
>
> *"And no sense is ever obtained, partly because only isolated beings*

---

[104] *The Tales, Ch XLIII. Beelzebub's Survey of the Process of the Periodic Reciprocal Destruction of Men, or Beelzebub's Opinion of War, p1069*

*there ponder over this matter, and partly thanks to the absence there, as is usual, of one common-planetary organization for a single line of action; and therefore, if even the mentioned isolated beings ponder over this question and constate something sensible about this horror, then this constating of theirs is never widely spread and fails to penetrate into the consciousness of other beings. And in addition, it is very sad about this 'sincere pondering' of the beings upon similar questions. I must tell you that thanks to the abnormally established conditions of being-existence there, the 'waking psyche' as it is expressed there, of each one of them gradually becomes from the very beginning of responsible existence such that he can 'think sincerely' and see things in the true light exclusively only if his stomach is so full of first being-food that it is impossible for what are called 'wandering nerves' in it to move, or, as they themselves say, he is 'stuffed quite full'; and besides, all his needs already inherent in him which are unbecoming to three-brained beings and which have become the dominant factors for the whole of his presence, are fully satisfied, of course, only for that given moment.*[105]

Because of the abnormal conditions of being-existence men are incapable of thinking sincerely for very long.

## In Summary

The abnormal conditions of being-existence in Man can be set side-by-side with the abnormal conditions of being-existence within ourselves.

In making such a comparison we are brought face-to-face with the difficulty that anyone who chooses to work on themselves faces: the finding of a source of true knowledge, the effort to ingest that knowledge, the subsequent decision to use that knowledge, the effort involved in using the knowledge (to suffer) in order to observe what one really is, and finally the effort to purge one's defects and move towards self-perfection. A great deal of this battle with mechanicality involves a struggle with the formatory apparatus and requires the

---

[105] *The Tales, Ch XLIII. Beelzebub's Survey of the Process of the Periodic Reciprocal Destruction of Men, or Beelzebub's Opinion of War, p1057*

assistance of a "teacher," someone who has themselves  escaped from this prison.

In *The Tales,* Beelzebub discusses the efforts of *messengers sent from above* to raise the level of humanity. This is characterized by Beelzebub as an effort to uproot the consequences of the properties of the organ Kundabuffer.

# CHAPTER VIII

# The Consequences of the Properties

*"There must be something to explain why we are all such fools; why we are not self-conscious; why we treat ourselves with such care. There is something: it is Kundabuffer.."*

*~ A. R. Orage*

Gurdjieff repeats the words "the consequences of the properties of the organ Kundabuffer" seventy times in *The Tales*. It is a hypnotic refrain that penetrates the mind of the reader. Nevertheless he does not say much about the impact of Kundabuffer directly. Instead the frequent mentions of Kundabuffer are made almost as side-comments in his telling of his many tales.

According to the text, the need for Kundabuffer is created by the splitting off of the two fragments of Earth: Moon and Anulios. The Most High Commission, having reviewed the situation, notes that, although the broken off fragments might maintain themselves in their existing positions, in future they might leave their position and become the cause of irreparable calamities. It concludes that the Earth needs to constantly send the scared vibrations 'Askokin' to the detached fragments. To ensure this necessary transmission they implant Kundabuffer in man. The text reads:

> *"So, my boy, in view of this the Most High Commission then de-cided among other things provisionally to implant into the com-mon presences of the three-brained beings there a special organ*

*with a property such that, first, they should perceive reality topsy-turvy and, secondly, that every repeated impression from outside should crystallize in them data which would engender factors for evoking in them sensations of 'pleasure' and 'enjoyment.'*[106]

Kundabuffer causes Man to see things "upside down" rather than to see reality as it is. The impressions men consume are filtered or buffered in some way. Specifically, when Kundabuffer operates, *"every repeated impression from outside"* crystallizes data in them that will *"engender factors for evoking in them sensations of 'pleasure' and 'enjoyment.'"*

Kundabuffer is implanted very early in the life of the embryo (when men have tails) and provides a foundation from which all repeated incoming impressions, no matter what they are, engender sensory pleasure.

The embryonic tail develops between 4 and 5 weeks of age, with the embryo having 10–12 developing tail vertebrae. By the 8th week of gestation, the sixth to twelfth tail vertebrae and the associated tissues have normally disappeared through a process of cell death. This occurs as the embryo gradually develops its nervous system.

Touch is the first sense to emerge at around 8 weeks, concentrated around the lips and nose. By 12 weeks the palms and soles have become touch sensitive. The senses of taste (via taste buds) and smell (olfactory nerves) emerge very soon after, with the baby able to experience variations in the taste of the amniotic fluid which is flavored according to the mother's diet. While smell is of little practical use within the womb, a baby is born able to recognize its mother's smell, especially the smell of the breast milk.

By 20 weeks, the hearing system is fully-developed. Babies can identify the voices of family members it has heard while it was in the womb. A fetus can also startle in response to loud sounds. The eyes begin to develop at about 7 weeks, and are almost fully formed just a few weeks later. However, the eyelids remain closed until about 27

---

[106] *The Tales, Ch X. Why "Men" are not Men, p88*

weeks. The fetus may then be able to detect light faintly through the walls of the womb.

Brain scans on unborn infants suggest that a fetus does not sense pain until after 30 weeks, when the somatosensory neural pathways finish developing. By the mid-third trimester, the baby is able to appreciate a full range of sensations, including heat, cold, pressure, and pain in every part of the body.

If the developing fetus doesn't experience pain for the first 30 weeks, then Gurdjieff's suggestion that *"every repeated impression from outside"* crystallizes data in them that will *"engender factors for evoking in them sensations of 'pleasure' and 'enjoyment.' "* appears to be biologically accurate. It may be the case that the organ Kundabuffer, which buffers all pain, is removed at around that time - or perhaps even earlier, when its influence has become habitual.

The Most High Commission visits the solar system on three occasions. On the first visit they gather data as to the situation after the collision of the comet Kondoor with the planet Earth, and consider what is to be done. On their second descent they implant the organ Kundabuffer in Man. The text reads:

> *"But nevertheless, my boy, this Most High Commission, having then calculated all the facts at hand, and also all that might happen in the future, came to the conclusion that although the fragments of the planet Earth might maintain themselves for the time being in their existing positions, yet in view of certain so-called 'Tastartoonarian-displacements' conjectured by the Commission, they might in the future leave their position and bring about a large number of irreparable calamities both for this system 'Ors' and for other neighboring solar systems.*[107]

Most likely "Tastartoonarian-displacements" refers to the contractions of the womb that give rise the the movement of the fetus (the moon) down the birth canal into the world. This is the only way, aside from caesarean delivery, that a fetus is ever displaced.

---

[107] *The Tales, Ch IX. The Cause of the Genesis of the Moon, p83*

Quite reasonably the Most High Commission concludes that the Earth (the mother of the Moon) should constantly feed its progeny. They are particularly convinced that this feeding should include the sacred substance Askokin.

> *"This sacred substance can be formed on planets only when both fundamental cosmic laws operating in them, the sacred 'Hepta-paraparshinokh' and the sacred 'Triamazikamno,' function, as is called, 'Ilnosoparno,' that is to say, when the said sacred cosmic laws in the given cosmic concentration are deflected independently and also manifest on its surface independently – of course independently only within certain limits.[108]*

It was thus necessary for this purpose to create the whole of nature. And that led to the appearance of corresponding beings (one, two and three-brained) who would be capable of producing the required sacred substance.

> *"And afterwards, when the said Sacred Individuals had obtained the sanction of HIS ENDLESSNESS for the actualization of the Ilnosoparnian process on that planet also, and when this process had been actualized under the direction of the same Great Archangel Sakaki, then from that time on, on that planet also, just as on many others, there began to arise the 'Corresponding,' owing to which the said detached fragments exist until now without constituting a menace for a catastrophe on a great scale.[109]*

The introjection of the organ Kundabuffer was a measure taken to ensure the production of the necessary amount of Askokin. However on the next visit of the Most High Commission, their investigations revealed that there was no longer any need for Kundabuffer.

> *"Meanwhile you must note that there was still a third descent of that Most High Commission to that planet, three years later according to objective time-calculations, but this time it was under the direction of the Most-Great-Arch-Seraph Sevohtartra, the Most Great Archangel Sakaki having, in the meantime, become worthy to become the divine Individual he now is, namely, one of the four Quarter-Maintainers of the whole Universe.*

---

[108] *The Tales, Ch IX. The Cause of the Genesis of the Moon, p84*
[109] *The Tales, IX. The Cause of the Genesis of the Moon, p84*

*"And during just this third descent there, when it was made clear by the thorough investigations of the sacred members of this third Most High Commission that for the maintenance of the existence of those said detached fragments there was no longer any need to continue to actualize the deliberately taken anticipatory measures, then among the other measures there was also destroyed, with the help of the same Arch-Chemist-Physicist Angel Looisos, in the presences of the three-brained beings there, the said organ Kundabuffer with all its astonishing properties.*

One of the major arcs of *The Tales* is the allegory of man's development through his life. Atlantis represents childhood, with the sinking of Atlantis representing the transapalnian displacement of essence, which was then the conscious part of the psyche, by personality, and essence becoming subconscious – sinking beneath the waves.

Beelzebub says:

*"It is necessary to premise just here that at the period of my first descent in person onto this planet, the organ Kundabuffer was no longer in the three-brained beings who interest you.*

*"And it was only in some of the three-brained beings there that various consequences of the properties of that for them maleficent organ had already begun to be crystallized.*

*"In the period to which this tale of mine refers, one of the consequences of the properties of this organ which had already become thoroughly crystallized in a number of beings there was that consequence of the property which, while the organ Kundabuffer itself was still functioning in them, had enabled them very easily and without any 'remorse-of-conscience' not to carry out voluntarily any duties taken upon themselves or given them by a superior. But every duty they fulfilled was fulfilled only from the fear and apprehension of 'threats' and 'menaces' from outside.*

*"It was in just this same consequence of this property already thoroughly crystallized in some beings of that period there, that the cause of this whole incident lay.*[110]

---

[110] *The Tales, Ch XV. The First Descent of Beelzebub upon the Planet Earth, p111*

It is from this part of *The Tales* that we start to become familiar with the maleficent influence of the habits that Kundabuffer conferred on us.

## Explicitly Listed Negative Qualities

From *The Tales* we can construct a comprehensive inventory of the negative manifestations that the consequences of the properties of the organ Kundabuffer bestow upon man. The following excerpts include such lists.

Early in the book when Beelzebub declares the chief particularity of men to be their periodic pursuit of the process of the destruction of each other's existence. He goes on to say:

> "Besides this chief particularity of their common psyche. there are completely crystallized in them and there unfailingly become a part of their common presences – regardless of where they may arise and exist – functions which exist under the names 'egoism,' 'self-love,' 'vanity,' 'pride,' 'self-conceit,' 'credulity,' 'suggestibility,' and many other properties quite abnormal and quite unbecoming to the essence of any three-brained beings whatsoever.

> "Of these abnormal being-particularities, the particularity of their psyche the most terrible for them personally is that which is called 'suggestibility.'[111]

When discussing Faith, Love and Hope in Man, Beelzebub remarks:

> "'The contemporary three-centered beings here do at times believe, love, and hope with their Reason as well as with their feelings; but how they believe, how they love, and how they hope – ah, it is exactly in this that all the peculiarity of these three being-properties lies!

> "'They also believe, but this sacred impulse in them does not function independently, as it does in general in all the three-centered beings existing on the various other planets of our Great Universe upon which beings with the same possibilities breed; but it arises dependent upon some or other factors, which have been formed in their common presences, owing as always to the same consequences

---

[111] *The Tales, Ch XIV. The Beginnings of Perspectives Promising Nothing Very Cheerful. p107*

*of the properties of the organ Kundabuffer – as for instance, the particular properties arising in them which they call "vanity," "self-love," "pride," "self-conceit," and so forth.*[112]

Slightly later in the book Beelzebub also says:

*"'The contemporary three-centered beings here do at times believe, love, and hope with their Reason as well as with their feelings; but how they believe, how they love, and how they hope – ah, it is exactly in this that all the peculiarity of these three being-properties lies!*

*"'They also believe, but this sacred impulse in them does not function independently, as it does in general in all the three-centered beings existing on the various other planets of our Great Universe upon which beings with the same possibilities breed; but it arises dependent upon some or other factors, which have been formed in their common presences, owing as always to the same consequences of the properties of the organ Kundabuffer – as or instance, the particular properties arising in them which they call "vanity," "self-love," "pride," "self-conceit," and so forth.*

*"'In consequence of this, the three-brained beings here are for the most part subject just to the perceptions and fixations in their presences of all sorts of "Sinkrpoosarams" or, as it is expressed here, they "believe-any-old-tale."*

*"'It is perfectly easy to convince beings of this planet of anything you like, provided only during their perceptions of these "fictions," there is evoked in them and there proceeds, either consciously from without, or automatically by itself, the functioning of one or another corresponding consequence of the properties of the organ Kundabuffer crystallized in them from among those that form what is called the "subjectivity" of the given being, as for instance: "self-love," "vanity," "pride," "swagger," "imagination," "bragging," "arrogance," and so on.*[113]

In discussing how the English conquered and proceeded to dominate the Indian subcontinent, which Beelzebub calls Gemchania, he says:

---

[112] *The Tales, Ch XXVI. The Legominism Concerning the Deliberations of the Very Saintly Ashiata Shiemash under the Title of "The Terror-of-the-Situation.", p356*

[113] *The Tales, Ch XXVII. The Organization for Man's Existence Created by the Very Saintly Ashiata Shiemash, p384*

*"These beings from different communities of Europe continued also to manifest there toward each other the kind of strange being-relationships which beings of one European community manifested then and still continue to manifest towards beings belonging to other communities of the same continent; namely, thanks also to the consequences of the properties of the organ Kundabuffer, they cultivate feelings which had been crystallized in them, into the forms of particular functions existing there under the names of, 'envy,' 'jealousy,' 'sandoor' (i.e., wishing the death or weakness of others), and so on.*[114]

In describing Lentrohamsanin, and remarking upon his lack of "Being" of that eternal hasnammus, Beelzebub says:

*"Well, when the said Mama's-and-Papa's-darling became a learned being there of new formation, then because on the one hand there was no Being whatsoever in his presence, and on the other hand because there had already by this time been thoroughly crystallized in him those consequences of the properties of the organ Kundabuffer which exist there under the names of 'vanity,' 'self-love,' 'swagger,' and so forth, the ambition arose in him to become a famous learned being not only among the beings of Nievia, but also over the whole of the surface of their planet.*[115]

In the following excerpt which relates to man's education Beelzebub asserts that these negative consequences of the properties of Kundabuffer actually become "organic functions":

*"Thanks to this abnormal education of theirs, not only is nothing crystallized in them to enable them to reflect and actualize anything effective in practice, but on the contrary, thanks to this abnormal education those many consequences of the properties of the for them accursed organ Kundabuffer devised by the great Angel, now already Archangel Looisos, are gradually formed in them and become organic functions, and, being transmitted by heredity from one generation to another, are in general crystallized in the psyche of these unfortunates.*

*"Namely, those consequences of the said organ are formed in them,*

---

[114] *The Tales, Ch XXXVIII. Religion, p719*

[115] *The Tales, Ch XXVIII. The Chief Culprit in the Destruction of All the Very Saintly Labors of Ashiata Shiemash, p394*

146

*which exist there today under the names of 'egoism,' 'partiality,' 'vanity,' 'self-love,' and so on.*[116]

While intervening in Beelzebub's review of contemporary art, (with Beelzebub's permission), Ahoon lists such qualities as he describes contemporary artists:

*"You must know that those beings who are assumed to be the adepts of this contemporary art which is adorned with a false halo are not only put on their own level by the other three-brained beings there of the contemporary civilization, particularly during the several latter decades, and imitated by them in their exterior manifestations, but they are always and everywhere undeservingly encouraged and exalted by them; and in these contemporary representatives of art themselves, who really in point of their genuine essence are almost nonentities, there is formed of itself without any of their being-consciousness a false assurance that they are not like all the rest but, as they entitle themselves, of a 'higher order,' with the result that in the common presences of these types the crystallization of the consequences of the properties of the organ Kundabuffer proceeds more intensively than in the presences of all the other three-brained beings there.*

*"Just in regard to such unfortunate three-brained beings the surrounding abnormal conditions of ordinary being-existence are already so established that there are bound to be crystallized in their common presences and to become an inseparable part of their general psyche those of the consequences of the organ Kundabuffer which they now themselves call 'swagger,' 'pride,' 'self-love,' 'vanity,' 'self-conceit,' 'self-enamoredness,' 'envy,' 'hate,' 'offensiveness,' and so on and so forth.*[117]

Speaking specifically about actors, Ahoon advises that if Hassein has for some reason to exist on Earth and have dealings with any actors he advises Hassein never to tell the truth to such people, saying:

*"To such terrestrial types you must always say to their face only such things as may 'tickle' those consequences of the properties of*

---

[116] *The Tales, Ch XLIII. Beelzebub's Survey of the Process of the Periodic Reciprocal Destruction of Men, or Beelzebub's Opinion of War, p1061*
[117] *The Tales, Ch XXX. Art, p512*

*the organ Kundabuffer unfailingly crystallized in them and which I have already enumerated, namely, 'envy,' 'pride,' 'self-love,' 'vanity,' 'lying,' and so on.*[118]

Finally, when discussing the recent American invention of "comfortable seats," he remarks that men generally believe that such inventions of theirs are being introduced for the first time, not even thinking that such inventions are in fact re-inventions. Beelzebub says:

> *"Thanks to this false conviction, the result of their strange mentation, and in addition, thanks to the effect on the totality of the functioning of their feelings, of the consequences of the properties of the organ Kundabuffer which inevitably arise in their presences at responsible age and which are called 'envy,' 'greed,' and 'jealousy,' it always happens there, that when the beings of any grouping become the possessors of anything which in the given period is considered desirable, in most cases because of that maleficent practice fixed in their everyday existence, which they express by the words 'not to cease progressing,' there immediately arises in the common presences of all the beings of other groupings, on whatever continents they may breed, as soon as the rumor of this reaches them, the desire to have the same, and from that moment, there arises in each of them firstly, the need to imitate them, and secondly, the 'indubitable certainty' that the beings of this other grouping must exist very correctly, since they have been able to acquire just what in the given period is accounted desirable.*

### The Full List of Consequences

The full list of the consequences of the properties of the organ Kundabuffer from above excerpts isas follows (in alphabetical order):

arrogance
bragging
credulity
envy
egoism

---

[118] *The Tales, Ch XXX. Art, p516*

greed

hate

imagination

jealousy

lying

offensiveness

partiality

pride

'sandoor' (i.e., wishing the death or weakness of others)

self-conceit

self-enamoredness

self-love

suggestibility

swagger

vanity

Curiously, it includes only four of the seven deadly sins, making no mention of sloth, lust and wrath.

## Crystallization

Gurdjieff makes it clear in several parts of *The Tales* that the consequences of the properties of the organ Kundabuffer are fully crystallized in man. He explains as follows:

> "*After a considerable time had passed it was suddenly revealed that, although all the properties of the said organ had indeed been removed from the presences of your ancestors by the mentioned Most Sacred Individuals, yet nevertheless, a certain lawfully flowing cosmic result, existing under the name of "predisposition," and arising in every more or less independent cosmic presence owing to the repeated action in it of any function, had not been foreseen and destroyed in their presences.*

> "*And so it turned out that owing to this predisposition, which began to pass by heredity to the succeeding generations, the consequences of many of the properties of the organ Kundabuffer began*

*gradually to be crystallized in their presences.*

*"'No sooner was this lamentable fact which proceeded in the presences of the three-brained beings breeding on this planet Earth first made clear, than by All-Gracious sanction of our COMMON FATHER, a suitable Sacred Individual was immediately sent here, so that, being coated with a presence like your own and having become perfected by Objective Reason under the conditions already established here, he might better explain and show you the way of eradicating from your presences the already crystallized consequences of the properties of the organ Kundabuffer as well as your inherited predispositions to new crystallizations.* [119]

Man's abnormal education exacerbates this process of crystallization.

> *"Thanks to this abnormal education of theirs, not only is nothing crystallized in them to enable them to reflect and actualize anything effective in practice, but on the contrary, thanks to this abnormal education those many consequences of the properties of the for them accursed organ Kundabuffer devised by the great Angel, now already Archangel Looisos, are gradually formed in them and become organic functions, and, being transmitted by heredity from one generation to another, are in general crystallized in the psyche of these unfortunates.* [120]

And in Ashiata Shiemash's legominism under the title of *The-Terror-Of-The-Situation*, he observes that this crystallization has occurred.

> *"'The different manifestations of the beings I then encountered, which increased my doubts, gradually convinced me that these consequences of the properties of the organ Kundabuffer, having passed by heredity through a series of generations over a very long period of time, had ultimately so crystallized in their presences, that they now reached contemporary beings already as a lawful part of their essence, and hence these crystallized consequences of the properties of the organ Kundabuffer are now, as it were, a "second na-*

---

[119] *The Tales, Ch XXI. The First Visit of Beelzebub to India, p237*

[120] *The Tales, Ch XLIII. Beelzebub's Survey of the Process of the Periodic Reciprocal Destruction of Men, or Beelzebub's Opinion of War, p1059*

*ture" of their common presences.*[121]

Here we learn that this crystallization has become part of our essence.

## The Genesis of the Hasnamuss

Possibly the most maleficent consequence of the properties of the organ kundabuffer is that some men descend to the level of what Beelzebub calls a "hasnamuss." Hasnamusses can be thought of as objectively criminal beings. Beelzebub describes such beings in the following words:

> *"Concerning the 'typicality' of the three-brained beings for whom I have adopted this verbal definition, I shall explain it to you at the proper time, but meanwhile know that this word designates every already 'definitized' common presence of a three-brained being, both those consisting only of the single planetary body as well as those whose higher being-bodies are already coated in them, and in which for some reason or other, data have not been crystallized for the Divine impulse of 'Objective-Conscience.' "*[122]

Put simply they are men with no trace of objective conscience. Beelzebub later lists the characteristics of such men:

> *"If these separate aspects of the entire 'spectrum' of Naloo-osnian-impulses are described according to the notions of your favorites and expressed in their language, they might then be defined as follows:*
>
> *(1) Every kind of depravity, conscious as well as unconscious*
>
> *(2) The feeling of self-satisfaction from leading others astray*
>
> *(3) The irresistible inclination to destroy the existence of other breathing creatures*
>
> *(4) The urge to become free from the necessity of actualizing the being-efforts demanded by Nature*
>
> *(5) The attempt by every kind of artificiality to conceal from others what in their opinion are one's physical defects*

---

[121] *The Tales, Ch XXVI. The Legominism Concerning the Deliberations of the Very Saintly Ashiata Shiemash under the Title of "The Terror-of-the-Situation.", p354*

[122] *The Tales, Ch XXI. The First Visit Of Beelzebub To India, p235*

*(6) The calm self-contentment in the use of what is not personally deserved*

*(7) The striving to be not what one is.* [123]

Beelzebub asserts that man's religions (Havatvernoni) have been one of the chief causes of the gradual dilution of their psyche. He says:

*"Such an, in the objective sense, indeed, 'archmaleficent' factor for the gradual automatic 'dwindling' of their psyche arose there, on this ill-starred planet, also since various consequences of the properties of always the same for them accursed organ Kundabuffer began to be crystallized in them, and changing its outer form, began to be transmitted from generation to generation.*

*"And so, when, on the one hand, thanks to these crystallizations, there began to be acquired in the common presences of certain terrestrial three-brained beings, the first germs of what are called Hasnamussian properties, in consequence of which such beings began, as is proper to them for their egoistic aims, to invent for the 'confusion' of surrounding beings similar to themselves, various fictions, among which were also every kind of fantastic, what are called 'religious teachings'; and when, on the other hand, other of your favorites began to have faith in these fantastic religious teachings, and gradually lost their 'sane mentation' thanks to these same crystallizations, then from that time on there began to arise in the process of the ordinary existence of these strange three-brained beings a large number of 'Havatvernoni' or 'religions' having nothing in common with each other.*[124]

Beelzebub suggests that early Hasnamuss individuals invented false religious teachings. The distortion of religious teaching by Hasnamussian individuals is a repeating theme throughout *The Tales*.

### Hasnamuss Cunning

While in Babylon, attending a conference of learned beings who are discussing "whether or not men have a soul," Beelzebub wit-

---

[123] *The Tales, Ch XXVIII. The Chief Culprit in the Destruction of All the Very Saintly Labors of Ashiata Shiemash, p405-406*

[124] *The Tales, Ch XXXVIII. Religion, p694*

nesses the speech of Hamolinadir on the topic of 'Instability-of-Human-Reason.' Telling the story of this, Beelzebub says:

> *"So that you may be able to put yourself in the place of that sympathetic Assyrian, I shall also explain to you that in general on your planet, then in the city of Babylon as well as at the present time, all the theories on such a question as they call it of 'the beyond,' or any other 'elucidation-of-details' of any definite 'fact,' are invented by those three-brained beings there in whom most of the consequences of the properties of the organ Kundabuffer are completely crystallized, in consequence of which there actively functions in their presence, that being-property, which they themselves call 'cunning.' Owing to this, they consciously – of course consciously only with the sort of reason which it has already become long ago proper for them alone to possess – and moreover, merely automatically, gradually acquire in their common presence the capacity for 'spotting' the weakness of the psyche of the surrounding beings like themselves; and this capacity gradually forms in them data which enable them at times to sense and even to understand the peculiar logic of the beings around them, and according to these data, they invent and propound one of their 'theories' concerning this or that question; and because, as I have already told you, in most of the three-brained beings there, owing to the abnormal conditions of ordinary being-existence established there by them themselves, the being-function called 'instinctively-to-sense-cosmic-truths' gradually atrophies, then, if any one of them happens to devote himself to the detailed study of any one of these 'theories,' he is bound, whether he wishes or not, to be persuaded by it with the whole of his presence."[125]*

So, Hasnamussian individuals become cunning at being able to mislead others. This is facilitated by the fact that men no longer instinctively sense cosmic truths; to put it simply, they are suggestible. Also Hasnamusses are skilled in acquiring power. Beelzebub explains:

> *"When, according to various chance circumstances, and wherever significant groups of them became concentrated and they exist together, then several of them – in whom firstly for some reason or other the consequences of the properties of the organ Kundabuffer*

---
[125] *The Tales, Ch XXIV. Beelzebub's Flight to the Planet Earth for the Fifth Time, p333-334*

*had been previously well crystallized, the totality of which crystal-
lizations in general gives to their common presences the impulses
for what is called 'cunning,' and secondly, in whose hands at the
given time there appear for some reason or other many different,
what are called 'terrifying means,' or what they themselves call
'weapons' – quickly set themselves apart from other beings and
putting themselves at their head, constitute the beginnings of what
are called the 'ruling class.'*[126]

## The Destruction of work people

According to Beelzebub, a particularly disturbing aspect of Hasnamussian behavior that accompanies violent revolutions is the delib-
erate and unnecessary destruction of beings who are pursuing a
spiritual path.

> *"It is extremely interesting to notice here one exceedingly astonish-
> ing and incomprehensible fact.*
>
> *"And that is that during their later revolutions of this kind, almost
> all the three-brained beings there or at least the overwhelming ma-
> jority who begin to fall into such a 'psychosis,' always destroy for
> some reason or other the existence of just such other beings like
> themselves, as have, for some reason or other, chanced to find them-
> selves more or less on the track of the means of becoming free from
> the crystallization in themselves of the consequences of the proper-
> ties of that maleficent organ Kundabuffer which unfortunately
> their ancestors possessed.*[127]

## The Subversion of Art

Just as there are Hasnamusses in the fields of Philosophy, Religion
and Science, they also arise in the field of Art. Beelzebub comments
on this, having first described how the origins of art lie within the
efforts made by genuine learned beings of previous times to record
important knowledge using various aspects of artistic endeavor.
Beelzebub explains as follows:

> *"And as regards this word art itself, upon which, thanks to the
> strangeness of their Reason, there has been 'piled up' during this*

---

[126] *The Tales, Ch XXXIV. Russia, p626*
[127] *The Tales, Ch XV. The First Descent of Beelzebub upon the Planet Earth, p119*

*time, as they themselves would say, 'devil-knows-what,' I must tell you that my special investigations regarding this word made it clear to me that when this word among the other words and separate expressions used by the learned beings of that time also began automatically to pass from generation to generation and chanced to get into the vocabulary of certain three-brained beings there, in whose presences, owing to various surrounding circumstances, the crystallizations of the consequences of the properties of the organ Kundabuffer proceeded in that sequence and 'reciprocal-action,' as a result of which they predisposed the arising in their common presences of data for the Being of Hasnamuss-individuals; then this said word for some reason or other happening to please just this kind of three-brained being there, they began using it for their egoistic aims, and gradually made from it that very something which, although it continues to consist of, as it is said, 'complete vacuity,' yet has gradually collected about itself a fairylike exterior, which now 'blinds' every one of these favorites of yours who keeps his attention on it only a little longer than usual.*[128]

### Hasnamussian Activity in Music

The Hasnamuss Chai-Yoo was given help by genuine initiated beings and became worthy to be taught about the great apparatus Lav-Merz-Nokh in detail. However his desire to be regarded as a scientist led him to wiseacre a theory of his own about sound and to produce a simplified instrument called 'King.' The consequence was the degradation of knowledge, as Beelzebub describes:

*"And so, although the theory 'wiseacred' by this Chai-Yoo also did not last very long, yet nevertheless this sound-producing instrument King constructed by him had become generally accessible owing to its simplicity; and in consequence of the fact that the result obtained from it during intentional action turned out to be very good and satisfactory for, so to say, the 'tickling' of many data crystallized in their common presences thanks to the consequences of the properties of the organ Kundabuffer – it began to pass automatically down from generation to generation.*[129]

---

[128] *The Tales, Ch XXX. Art, p493*
[129] *The Tales, Ch XL. Beelzebub Tells How People Learned and Again Forgot about the Fundamental Cosmic Law of Heptaparaparshinokh, p855*

## The List of Hasnamusses

Aside from Chai-Yoo, mentioned above, the notable Hasnamuss individuals identified by Beelzebub include:

1) Lentrohamsanin, who inscribed his ideas on his famous Kashireitleer, and who is the chief culprit in the destruction of the labors of Ashiata Shiemash.

2) Harnahoom, who first suggested the idea that base metals could be transformed into gold by means of some secret process.

3) Alexander of Macedonia (or Alexander the Great), who conquered a vast region of The Middle East and Asia, destroying the Persian Empire of the day.

4) James Braid (Brade[130]), initially a follower of Mesmer, is now officially credited with being the "father of hypnosis," participated in "pecking Mesmer to death."

5) Armanatoora, the Tikliamishian priest who invented the religious teaching which insists (wrongly) that external "Good and Evil" exist.

# The Genesis of Objective Science

Only once in *The Tales* does Beelzebub relate how men made efforts of their own accord to eradicate the consequences of the properties of the organ Kundabuffer from their presences. This occurred at the time of Atlantis, and was led by Belcultassi. Beelzebub relates:

> *"... Belcultassi was once contemplating, according to the practice of every normal being, and his thoughts were by association concentrated on himself, that is to say, on the sense and aim of his existence, he suddenly sensed and cognized that the process of the functioning of the whole of him had until then proceeded not as it should have proceeded according to sane logic.[131]*

Belcultassi decided to try to confirm, discreetly, whether this defect in himself was also present in others.

---

[130] Gurdjieff deliberately misspells the surname Braid as Brade, possibly because the word "brade" means "to sell off or sell out" in French.

[131] The Tales, Ch XXIII, Beelzebub's Fourth Sojourn On The Earth, p233

*"Now among these friends and acquaintances of Belcultassi, there were several earnest beings who were not yet entirely slaves to the action of the consequences of the properties of the organ Kundabuffer, and who, having penetrated to the gist of the matter also became very seriously interested in it and began to verify that which proceeded in themselves, and independently to observe those around them.[132]*

The group which coalesced round Belcultassi became the learned society Akhaldan, the goal of which was *'The striving to become aware of the sense and aim of the Being of beings.'* Beelzebub continues to relate:

*"The three-brained beings of your planet who became members of this society actually did a great deal in respect of approaching objective knowledge which had never been done there before and which perhaps will never be repeated.*

*"And here it is impossible not to express regret and to repeat that to the most great misfortune of all terrestrial three-brained beings of all later epochs, it was just then—when after incredible being-labors by members of that great society the required tempo of work had already been established with regard to discernment, conscious on their part, and also with regard to their unconscious preparation for the welfare of their descendants—that, in the heat of it all, certain of them constated, as I have already told you, that something serious was to occur to their planet in the near future.[133]*

What then occurred was the second transapalnian perturbation and the sinking of Atlantis. The Akhaldan society survived and eventually established itself in Egypt. It was from that time onwards that mankind began to degenerate.

## Messengers Sent From Above

Beelzebub introduces the idea that occasionally, at the behest of the Absolute, a sacred individual is born on Earth with the intention that he will assist men in eliminating the consequences of Kundabuffer.

---

[132] *The Tales, Ch XXIII, Beelzebub's Fourth Sojourn On The Earth, p297*
[133] *The Tales, Ch XXIII, Beelzebub's Fourth Sojourn On The Earth, p300*

*"Before continuing to tell you about the three-brained beings breeding just on that part of the surface of the planet Earth, it is, I think, necessary to remark, even if briefly, that there existed and still exist, ever since the time when the practice of having peculiar being-Havatvernonis or Religions began to arise and exist among your favorites, two basic kinds of religious-teachings.*

*"One kind was invented by those three-brained beings there themselves, in whom, for some reason or other, there arises the functioning of a psyche proper to Hasnamusses; and the other kind of religious-teaching is founded there upon those detailed instructions which have been preached, as it were, by genuine Messengers from Above, who indeed are from time to time sent by certain nearest helpers of our COMMON FATHER, for the purpose of aiding the three-brained beings of your planet in destroying in their presences the crystallized consequences of the properties of the organ Kundabuffer.[134]*

However as Beelzebub explains, their efforts have not made a lasting difference.

*"During these long centuries many sacred Individuals have been sent down to them here from Above with the special aim of helping them to deliver themselves from the consequences of the properties of the organ Kundabuffer, yet nevertheless nothing has changed here and the whole process of ordinary being-existence has remained as before.[135]*

## Buddha

Buddha is the first sacred individual sent from above that Beelzebub speaks about. Buddha decided to fulfil his allotted task by means of enlightening men's Reason – even though the Reason of the three-centered beings of Earth was, at the time, abnormally formed and functioned only through corresponding shocks from without.

The Buddha explains to a group of his initiates the implanting of Kundabuffer in man, and its consequences and then teaches them

---

[134] *The Tales, Ch XXI, The First Visit Of Beelzebub To India, p233*
[135] *The Tales, Ch XXXVII. France, p674*

what they need to know to attempt to eradicate its influence. Beelze-bub notes that he was, initially, successful.

> "*During the period when the said Sacred Individual, coated with a presence like your own and who had already attained to the age of a responsible three-centered being similar to yourselves, directly guided the ordinary process of the being-existence of your ancestors, many of them did indeed completely free themselves from the consequences of the properties of the organ Kundabuffer and either thereby acquired Being personally for themselves or became normal sources for the arising of normal presences of succeeding beings similar to themselves.*

> "*But in consequence of the fact that before the period of the said Sacred Individual's appearance here, the duration of your existence had, owing to very many firmly fixed abnormal conditions of ordinary existence created by yourselves, already become abnormally short, and therefore the process of sacred Rascooarno had also very soon to occur to this Sacred Individual, that is to say, he also had, like you, to die prematurely, then after his death, the former conditions were gradually re-established there owing on the one hand to the established abnormal conditions of ordinary being-existence and, on the other hand, to that maleficent particularity in your psyche, called Wiseacring.*

> "*Owing to this said particularity in your psyche, the beings here already of the second generation after the contemporaries of the mentioned Sacred Individual who had been sent from Above began gradually to change everything he had explained and indicated, and the whole of it was finally completely destroyed.*[136]

The teachings of Saint Buddha were thus destroyed completely by Wiseacring. The same fate attended the teachings of Saint Moses.

## Moses

Beelzebub describes this as follows:

> "*This Sacred Individual, whom your favorites at the present time call 'Saint Moses,' accomplished a great deal for them and left them many of those exact and corresponding indications for ordinary existence, so that if they would adopt and actualize them normally,*

---
[136] *The Tales, Ch XXI, The First Visit Of Beelzebub To India, p238*

*then, indeed, all the consequences of the properties of the absolutely maleficent for them organ Kundabuffer might become gradually decrystallized, and even the predisposition for new crystallizations might be destroyed.*

*"But to the common misfortune of all beings, with just a little Reason, of all our Great Universe, they began gradually to mix into all the counsels and indications of this 'normality-loving' Saint Moses, as it was already proper to them to do, such a mass of what are called 'spices,' that the saintly author himself could not with all his wish recognize anything of his own in this, as it were, totality collected by them of all he had explained and indicated.*[137]

## *Jesus Christ*

Beelzebub points to the demonizing of Judas as an example of the distortion of the teachings of Christ. Speaking of Judas he says:

*"But in fact, this Judas was not only the most faithful and devoted of all the near followers of Jesus Christ, but also, only thanks to his Reason and presence of mind all the acts of this Sacred Individual could form that result, which if it did not serve as the basis for the total destruction of the consequences of the properties of the organ Kundabuffer in these unfortunate three-brained beings, yet it was nevertheless, during twenty centuries the source of nourishment and inspiration for the majority of them in their desolate existence and made it at least a little endurable.*[138]

He also relates that Christ's teachings were preserved in a pure form by the Essenes.

*"By the way, I may tell you here that among a rather small group of terrestrial beings the teaching of Jesus Christ was preserved unchanged, and, passing from generation to generation, has even reached the present time in its original form.*

*"This smallish group of terrestrial beings is designated 'the Brotherhood of the Essenes.' The beings of this brotherhood succeeded at first in introducing the teaching of this Divine Teacher into their own being-existence, and subsequently in transmitting it from generation to generation to later generations, as a very good means for*

---

[137] *The Tales, Ch XXXVIII. Religion, p700*
[138] *The Tales, Ch XXXVIII. Religion, p740*

*freeing themselves from the consequences of the properties of the organ Kundabuffer..*[139]

## Mohammed

The distortion of Islam was also in part due to wiseacring. Beelzebub says:

> *"Now as regards the fourth great religion existing there now, which arose several centuries after the Christian religion, and was founded on the teaching of the full-of-hope Saint Mohammed, this religion at first spread there widely: and it might perhaps have become eventually a 'hearth of hope and reconciliation' for them all if these strange beings had not stirred this also into a hotchpotch.*
>
> *"On the one hand its followers also mixed into it something from the fantastic theory of the Babylonian dualists, but, on the other hand, the 'elders of the church' of this religion, called in this case 'Sheiks-Islamists,' themselves invented and added to it many things about the blessings of the notorious 'paradise,' which as it were, existed 'in the other world,' such blessings as perhaps could never even have entered the head of the chief Governor of Purgatory, His All-Quarters-Maintainer the Archcherub Helkgematios, even if he were deliberately to try to imagine them.*[140]

He then proceeds to describe the unfortunate schism between the Sunni and Shiite sects of Islam which persists unto this day.

## Saint Lama

The known history of the origination and development of Tibetan religion does not clearly identify a single individual as its founder and inspiration. Beelzebub asserts that there was such an individual whom he calls Saint Lama. He relates:

> *"Now let us talk about what I promised to tell you a little more in detail, namely, about the teachings of the last Sacred Individual who appeared among the beings of Tibet, Saint Lama, and about the causes of the complete destruction of that teaching also.*
>
> *"The teaching and preachings of this Saint were not so widely*

---

[139] *The Tales, Ch XXXVIII. Religion, p703-704*
[140] *The Tales, Ch XXXVIII. Religion, p704*

*spread there, because of the geographical conditions of that locality where he appeared, and where he taught those unfortunate three-centered beings also what they must do to free themselves from the consequences of the properties of the organ Kundabuffer.*

*"On account of its geographical conditions, beings of this country were little in touch, as I have already told you, with the abnormal conditions of ordinary being-existence of the beings of other communities, and in consequence certain of them were more receptive of the teaching of this last Sacred Individual, and this teaching therefore just entered into their essence and began gradually to be actualized already in practice also.*

*"So, my boy, during many years there circumstances gradually so arranged themselves in that country called Tibet, that the local beings became grouped according to the degree of their inner transubstantiation of the teaching of this Saint Lama, and according to the degree of their need to work upon themselves; and having correspondingly organized their ordinary existence, they, thanks to their isolated environment due to this inaccessibility of their country for beings of other communities, had the possibility of working, without hindrance according to the instructions of Saint Lama, upon their liberation from the consequences of the properties of that organ which their first, earliest ancestors, to their common misfortune, were forced to have.*[141]

Beelzebub then describes how the British invasion of Tibet destroyed a the existence of a group of seven Tibetans who had perfected themselves to a high level and who served as repositories of knowledge. He explains:

*"This group consisted of these seven beings who, following the indications of Saint Lama for freeing themselves from the consequences of the properties of the organ Kundabuffer, had brought their self-perfecting up to the final degree.*[142]

The group of seven were destroyed because, first of all, their leader was killed by a stray bullet fired from the British Expeditionary force - and the other six were destroyed because a ritual they performed to try to communicate with the Kesdjan body of their leader went

---

[141] *The Tales, Ch XXXVIII. Religion, p715-716*
[142] *The Tales, Ch XXXVIII. Religion, p721*

badly wrong - destroying both the six and also a library of information they had assembled.

*"And so, my boy, it has now become clear to you how there on your planet all the five religions I named, still remaining there at the present time and which were founded on the teachings of five different genuine saints sent to the three-brained beings from Above for helping them to free themselves from the consequences of the properties of the organ Kundabuffer, how, although all these five religions have gradually become changed, thanks as always to the same conditions of ordinary being-existence abnormally established just by them, until they were eventually turned for any sane mentation into children's fairy tales, yet nevertheless these five religions still served for some of them as a support for these inner moral motives, owing to which during certain previous periods, their mutual existence became more or less becoming to three-centered beings.*

## Ashiata Shiemash

One of the pupils of Louise March has the following recollection of a meeting she attended:

*Louise March related something which took place while she was working directly with Gurdjieff translating 1st Series into German. They were working on the passage with Ashiata Shiemash. During the reading of the material, Gurdjieff very earnestly engaged with Louise, pressing her for an answer:*

*"You believe? You believe Ashiata Shiemash?"*

*Louise pondered the question for a few moments, taken aback, then answered him by saying, "Yes. I believe he was real."*

*"Not was," replied Gurdjieff sternly. "Will Be!"*[143]

This accords with the opinion that a number of readers of *The Tales* have expressed: that Ashiata Shiemash is, metaphorically, Gurdjieff or alternatively that Gurdjieff was the forerunner for Ashiata Shiemash, who may have already been born.

In introducing Ashiata Shiemash, Beelzebub says:

*"I have already more than once told you, that by the All Most Gra-*

---

[143] *Related privately by a pupil of Louise March.*

*cious Command of Our OMNI-LOVING COMMON FA-*
*THER ENDLESSNESS, our Cosmic Highest Most Very Saintly*
*Individuals sometimes actualize within the presence of some terres-*
*trial three-brained being, a 'definitized' conception of a sacred Indi-*
*vidual in order that he, having become a terrestrial being with such*
*a presence, may there on the spot 'orientate' himself and give to the*
*process of their ordinary being-existence such a corresponding new*
*direction, thanks to which the already crystallized consequences of*
*the properties of the organ Kundabuffer, as well as the predisposi-*
*tions to such new crystallizations, might perhaps be removed from*
*their presences.*[144]

Ashiata's deliberations on the situation of Man are articulated in
the Legominism he wrote under the Title of "The Terror-of-the-Situation."

In this Legominism he states:

*"'All the sacred Individuals here before me, specially and intention-*
*ally actualized from Above, have always endeavored while striving*
*for the same aim to accomplish the task laid upon them through*
*one or other of those three sacred ways for self-perfecting, foreor-*
*dained by OUR ENDLESS CREATOR HIMSELF, namely,*
*through the sacred ways based on the being-impulses called "Faith,"*
*"Hope," and "Love."*

One of the reasons why it seems sensible to consider Ashiata as a
"future sacred individual" is his comments about Faith, Hope and
Love.  In his Legominism he states:

*"'During the period of my year of special observations on all of*
*their manifestations and perceptions, I made it categorically clear*
*to myself that although the factors for engendering in their pres-*
*ences the sacred being-impulses of Faith, Hope, and Love are al-*
*ready quite degenerated in the beings of this planet, nevertheless, the*
*factor which ought to engender that being-impulse on which the*
*whole psyche of beings of a three-brained system is in general based,*
*and which impulse exists under the name of Objective-Conscience,*
*is not yet atrophied in them, but remains in their presences almost*
*in its primordial state.*

---

[144] *The Tales, Ch XXV. The Very Saintly Ashiata Shiemash, Sent from Above to the Earth, p347*

## Faith, Hope and Love

In his legominism, Ashiata writes the following about love:

> *"'In the presences of the beings of contemporary times, there also arises and is present in them as much as you please of that strange impulse which they call love; but this love of theirs is firstly also the result of certain crystallized consequences of the properties of the same Kundabuffer; and secondly this impulse of theirs arises and manifests itself in the process of every one of them entirely subjectively; so subjectively and so differently that if ten of them were asked to explain how they sensed this inner impulse of theirs, then all ten of them – if, of course, they for once replied sincerely, and frankly confessed their genuine sensations and not those they had read about somewhere or had obtained from somebody else – all ten would reply differently and describe ten different sensations.*[145]

And further

> *"'Thanks to this kind of love in the contemporary beings here, their hereditary predispositions to the crystallizations of the consequences of the properties of the organ Kundabuffer are crystallized at the present time without hindrance, and finally become fixed in their nature as a lawful part of them.*[146]

About hope he writes:

> *"'And as regards the third sacred being-impulse, namely, "essence-hope," its plight in the presences of the three-centered beings here is even worse than with the first two [faith and love].*

> *"'Such a being-impulse has not only finally adapted itself in them to the whole of their presences in a distorted form, but this maleficent strange "hope" newly formed in them, which has taken the place of the being-impulse of Sacred Hope, is now already the principal reason why factors can no longer be acquired in them for the functioning of the genuine being-impulses of Faith, Love, and Hope.*

> *"'In consequence of this newly-formed-abnormal hope of theirs, they always hope in something; and thereby all those possibilities are constantly being paralyzed in them, which arise in them either*

---

[145] *The Tales, Ch XXVI. The Legominism Concerning the Deliberations of the Very Saintly Ashiata Shiemash under the Title of "The Terror-of-the-Situation.", p357*

[146] *The Tales, Ch XXVI. The Legominism Concerning the Deliberations of the Very Saintly Ashiata Shiemash under the Title of "The Terror-of-the-Situation.", p358*

*intentionally from without or accidentally by themselves, which possibilities could perhaps still destroy in their presences their hereditary predispositions to the crystallizations of the consequences of the properties of the organ Kundabuffer.*[147]

Beelzebub draws our attention to a marble in the possession of the Brotherhood-Olbogmek on which the following Ashiatian inscription was found:

*"'Faith,' 'Love', and 'Hope'*

*Faith of consciousness is freedom*
*Faith of feeling is weakness*
*Faith of body is stupidity.*

*Love of consciousness evokes the same in response*
*Love of feeling evokes the opposite*
*Love of body depends only on type and polarity.*

*Hope of consciousness is strength*
*Hope of feeling is slavery*
*Hope of body is disease.*[148]

It would seems from these words that faith, hope and love in Man can be redeemed. However, the forward path is through conscience.

## The Ashiatian Organization

According to Beelzebub, Ashiata organized the brotherhood Heechtvori,[149] within which any brother could become an All-the-rights-possessing brother when he became able to convince a hundred other beings that the impulse of being-objective-conscience existed in man, and how it could manifested so that a Man could pursue the real sense and aim of his existence. The initial brotherhood would give rise to groups which would spawn other groups and thus this teaching would spread across the Earth.

---

[147] *The Tales, Ch XXVI. The Legominism Concerning the Deliberations of the Very Saintly Ashiata Shiemash under the Title of "The Terror-of-the-Situation.", p358-359*

[148] *The Tales, Ch XXVI. The Legominism Concerning the Deliberations of the Very Saintly Ashiata Shiemash under the Title of "The Terror-of-the-Situation.", p361*

[149] *Heechtvori means Only-he-will-be-called-and-will-become-the-Son-of-God-who-acquires-in-himself-Conscience*

It met with success. At the heart of the teaching was a set of five strivings, which Beelzebub describes in the following way:

*"All the beings of this planet then began to work in order to have in their consciousness this Divine function of genuine conscience, and for this purpose, as everywhere in the Universe, they transubstantiated in themselves what are called the 'being-obligolnian-strivings' which consist of the following five, namely:*

*"The first striving: to have in their ordinary being-existence everything satisfying and really necessary for their planetary body.*

*"The second striving: to have a constant and unflagging instinctive need for self-perfection in the sense of being.*

*"The third: the conscious striving to know ever more and more concerning the laws of World-creation and World-maintenance.*

*"The fourth: the striving from the beginning of their existence to pay for their arising and their individuality as quickly as possible, in order afterwards to be free to lighten as much as possible the Sorrow of our COMMON FATHER.*

*"And the fifth: the striving always to assist the most rapid perfecting of other beings, both those similar to oneself and those of other forms, up to the degree of the sacred 'Martfotai,' that is, up to the degree of self-individuality.*

*"At this period when every terrestrial three-centered being existed and worked consciously upon himself in accordance with these five strivings, many of them thanks to this quickly arrived at results of objective attainments perceptible to others.*[150]

## The Chapter In Summary

A simple way to study the consequences of the properties of the organ Kundbuffer is to ponder the list of consequences that Beelzebub mentions: arrogance, bragging, credulity, envy, egoism, greed, hate, imagination, jealousy, lying, offensiveness, partiality, pride, self-conceit, self-enamoredness, self-love, suggestibility, swagger and vanity.

---

[150] *The Tales, Ch XXVII. The Organization for Man's Existence Created by the Very Saintly Ashiata Shiemash, p386*

167

Beelzebub asserts that these consequences are crystallized within us when we are born,[151] and thus it is necessary for anyone who works on themselves to struggle with such states or manifestations.

The consequence of not doing so is to risk becoming a candidate for Hasnamuss. The development of Hasnamusses is a natural consequence of the properties of the organ Kundabuffer.

Historically, there are scant examples of men who have realized man's parlous situation without the help of a teacher – Belcultassi being the only individual who Beelzebub mentions in this regard. However there have been a succession of individuals who have appeared from time to time, sent from above with the goal of helping Man to eradicate the consequences of the properties of the organ Kundabuffer.

Over time the force of the teachings of each of the messengers sent from above declined, often through the wiseacring of followers. The latest of the messengers is Ashiata Shiemash, (the once and future messenger) for whom Gurdjieff is possibly the forerunner.

His teachings emphasize the awakening of objective conscience and included within them are the Five Obligolnian Strivings.

---

[151] *The Tales, Ch XXI. The First Visit of Beelzebub to India, p237*

# CHAPTER IX

## A Life For A Life

*"With thorns in the inner world there will always be roses in the outer world in law-able compensation."*
*~ Gurdjieff*

In theory, there are many things that man could do to reverse the decline that engulfed his species. Many of his negative traits stem from the abnormal conditions of being-existence, for which he himself is responsible, and these could perhaps be gradually turned in the direction of greater sanity.

These abnormal conditions of being-existence are the formatory apparatus of mankind. As with the formatory apparatus in any individual, there are good habits and bad. But in recent centuries, it is the negative side that has grown. There is a disharmony between Man and Nature which Man currently shows little sign of correcting. The internal organization of our species, in respect of national and international government, religion and education, offers immense scope for improvement, but evidence of improvement is hard to find.

Man's so-called "progress," although it has one or two positive aspects, has resulted in a society where all the natural functions of Man have gradually been subjugated by automation. This began in earnest with the advent of the industrial revolution, which has for centuries laid waste to craftsmanship. Machines have consumed the skills of man's moving center – carpentry, masonry, ironwork, pottery, etc.

The era of the horse as the engine of transport declined with the advent of the steam engine and came to an end with the advent of the automobile. The discovery of electricity and the subsequent invention of generators and electric motors moved machinery into the realm of electricity. Physical labor has been usurped by mechanical labor.

The emotional life of Man has been similarly whittled down. Fewer people attend church to sing and pray. The ranks of musicians, singers, actors, performers, artists and entertainers, have been decimated by the advent of mass media. It began with the phonograph and tape recorder and exploded from there. People became passive observers rather than participants in artistic endeavor. Even the pleasure of social interactions has diminished since the advent of the Internet.

We entered the digital age, and a global army of computers commandeered the intellectual life of man. It now presides over a vast ocean of data, all literature, all published writings and almost all our personal communications. Artificial Intelligence now stalks all intellectual activity, subsuming all calculation and a great of logical thinking in research, planning and design.

The human psyche has become the passive witness of its own surrender, in all its three lower centers. Mankind's formatory apparatus, his abnormal conditions of being-existence, have been thoroughly carved into silicon. Man's use of electricity has shortened the active life of man.

It seems then that mankind's spiritual decline is recent, and Beelzebub would concur. When explaining that  men no longer see Anulios, he remarks:

> *"Let us give them their due; during recent centuries they have really most artistically mechanized themselves to see nothing real.*[152]

---

[152] *The Tales, .Ch XLI. The Bokharian Dervish Hadi-Asvatz-Troov, p902*

Again, when explaining that contemporary theaters improve the quality of man's sleep, he says:

*"After the need to actualize being-Partkdolg-duty in themselves had entirely disappeared from the presences of most of them, and every kind of association of unavoidably perceived shocks began to proceed in the process of their waking state only from several already automatized what are called 'series-of-former-imprints' consisting of endlessly repeated what are called 'impressions-experienced-long-ago,' there then began to disappear in them and still continues to disappear even the instinctive need to perceive every kind of new shock vital for three-brained beings, and which issue either from their inner separate spiritualized being-parts or from corresponding perceptions coming from without for conscious associations, for just those being-associations upon which depends the intensity in the presences of beings of the transformation of every kind of 'being-energy.'*

*"During the latter three centuries the process itself of their existence has become such that in the presences of most of them during their daily existence those 'being-confrontative-associations' almost no longer arise, which usually proceed in three-brained beings thanks to every kind of new perception, and from which alone can data be crystallized in the common presences of three-brained beings for their own individuality.*[153]

Theoretically there are many things that Man could do to reverse the decline of his species, but ordinary man will never do any of them.

### The Disease of Tomorrow

Perhaps one of the most poignant passages in the whole of *The Tales* is where Beelzebub explains the disease of tomorrow. His Final words on this are as follows:

*"Owing to the said maleficent disease 'tomorrow' most of those unfortunate beings there who accidentally or owing to a conscious influence from without, become aware through their Reason in them of their complete nullity and begin to sense it with all their separate spiritualized parts, and who also chance to learn which and in*

---

[153] *The Tales, .Ch XLI. The Bokharian Dervish Hadi-Asvatz- Troov, p902*

*what way, being-efforts must be made in order to become such as it is proper for three-brained beings to be, also, by putting off from 'tomorrow' till 'tomorrow,' almost all arrive at the point that on one sorrowful day for themselves, there arise in them and begin to be manifest those forerunners of old age called 'feebleness' and 'infirmity,' which are the inevitable lot of all cosmic formations great and small toward the end of their completed existence.*

*"Here I must without fail tell you also about that strange phenomenon which I constated there during my observations and studies of the almost entirely degenerated presences of those favorites of yours; namely, I definitely constated that in many of them, toward the end of their planetary existence, most of the consequences of the properties of that same organ which had become crystallized in their common presences begin to atrophy of their own accord and some of them even entirely disappear, in consequence of which these beings begin to see and sense reality a little better.*

*"In such cases a strong desire appears in the common presences of such favorites of yours, to work upon themselves, to work as they say, for the 'salvation-of-their-soul.'*

*"But needless to say, nothing can result from such desires of theirs just because it is already too late for them, the time given them for this purpose by Great Nature having already passed; and although they see and feel the necessity of actualizing the required being-efforts, yet for the fulfillment of such desires of theirs, they have now only ineffectual yearnings and the 'lawful-infirmities-of-old-age.'*[154]

## Itoklanoz

From the perspective of The Work, mankind does not even see what the problem is. It is mankind's destiny to participate in the feeding of the Moon.

Mankind could have done this willingly if sufficient numbers of men had devoted themselves to being-Partkdolg-duty – conscious labors and intentional suffering. But mankind failed to do so, and as a consequence Nature began to actualize men according to the Itok-

---

[154] *The Tales, Ch XXVI. The Legominism Concerning the Deliberations of the Very Saintly Ashiata Shiemash under the Title of "The Terror-of-the-Situation.", p363*

lanoz principle,[155] ensuring that the Moon would be fed the necessary Askokin by men's death.

Clearly, ordinary men have no idea that this is their lot and they might not believe it even if it were possible to prove. For their own benefit they need to become aware of their slavery, and the only hope for this is through the actions of messengers from above.

In his Legominism, *The Terror of the Situation*, **Ashiata Shiemash relates:**

> *"'During the period of my year of special observations on all of their manifestations and perceptions, I made it categorically clear to myself that although the factors for engendering in their presences the sacred being-impulses of Faith, Hope, and Love are already quite degenerated in the beings of this planet, nevertheless, the factor which ought to engender that being-impulse on which the whole psyche of beings of a three-brained system is in general based, and which impulse exists under the name of Objective-Conscience, is not yet atrophied in them, but remains in their presences almost in its primordial state.*

> *"'Thanks to the abnormally established conditions of external ordinary being-existence existing here, this factor has gradually penetrated and become embedded in that consciousness which is here called "subconsciousness," in consequence of which it takes no part whatever in the functioning of their ordinary consciousness.*

> *"'Well, then, it was just then that I indubitably understood with all the separate ruminating parts representing the whole of my "I," that if the functioning of that being-factor still surviving in their common presences were to participate in the general functioning of that consciousness of theirs in which they pass their daily, as they here say, "waking-existence," only then would it still be possible to save the contemporary three-brained beings here from the consequences of the properties of that organ which was intentionally implanted into their first ancestors.[156]*

---

[155] *See The Tales, p131*

[156] *The Tales, Ch XXVI. The Legominism Concerning the Deliberations of the Very Saintly Ashiata Shiemash under the Title of "The Terror-of-the-Situation.", p359*

So Ashiata focussed on the creation of conditions that would enable the "sacred-conscience" buried in man's subconscious to enter into his ordinary consciousness. He organized a brotherhood called the Heechtvori, a name which signified 'Only-he-will-be-called-and-will-become-the-Son-of-God-who-acquires-in-himself-Conscience.' His intention was first to to raise his acolytes to a level where "sacred conscience" did indeed participate in their ordinary consciousness and then use them to enable that in others. Beelzebub explains:

> "According to the statutes drawn up by the Very Saintly Ashiata Shiemash, any brother could become an All-the-rights-possessing brother of the brotherhood Heechtvori, only when in addition to the other also foreseen definite objective attainments, he could bring himself—in the sense of 'ableness-of-conscious-direction-of-the-functioning-of-his-own-psyche'—to be able to know how to convince to perfection a hundred other beings and to prove to them that the impulse of being-objective-conscience exists in man, and secondly how it must be manifested in order that a man may respond to the real sense and aim of his existence, and moreover so to convince them that each of these others, in their turn, should acquire in themselves what is called the 'Required-intensity-of-ableness,' to be able to convince and persuade not less than a hundred others also.[157]

After Gurdjieff's death in 1949, many of his direct pupils set up groups who met regularly to "work on themselves" and this persisted for decades, until all of those direct pupils had themselves died. While it was clearly the intention of those group leaders to pass on what they could, and many proved to be inspirational to their pupils in their own right, the proliferation of Work ideas and activities that ensued does not conform to the hundred-to-one spread of being-objective-conscience that Ashiata Shiemash hoped for.

To break the lock that the consequences of the properties of the organ Kundabuffer has on mankind will require a force of that strength.

---

[157] *The Tales, Ch XXVI. The Legominism Concerning the Deliberations of the Very Saintly Ashiata Shiemash under the Title of "The Terror-of-the-Situation."*, p369

## The Dénoument

The Tales concludes with the ceremony that sanctifies the efforts that Beelzebub has made during his exile and reveals the gradation of Reason he has achieved. The ceremony deeply affects both Ahoon and Hassein. Once it is over, Beelzebub asks them both to take their usual places noting that before the Karnak arrives at its mooring place, there is yet a little time to talk. He therefore asks if Hassein has any question in mind that he could now address. Hassein responds:

*"Sacred Podkoolad, and cause of the cause of my arising.*

*"In order that the convictions formed in me during this time, owing to Your explanation of the abnormalities proceeding on the Earth, may become definitely crystallized in me, I still wish very much to have this time Your personal and frank opinion as to the following: How You would reply if, let us suppose, our ALL-EMBRACING CREATOR ENDLESSNESS HIMSELF, were to summon You before HIM and ask You this:*

*"'Beelzebub!!!!*

*"'You, as one of the anticipated, accelerated results of all My actualizations, manifest briefly the sum of your long-centuried impartial observations and studies of the psyche of the three-centered beings arising on the planet Earth and state in words whether it is still possible by some means or other to save them and to direct them into the becoming path?'"*[158]

Beelzebub's response is as follows:

*"The sole means now for the saving of the beings of the planet Earth would be to implant again into their presences a new organ, an organ like Kundabuffer, but this time of such properties that every one of these unfortunates during the process of existence should constantly sense and be cognizant of the inevitability of his own death as well as of the death of everyone upon whom his eyes or attention rests.*

*"Only such a sensation and such a cognizance can now destroy the egoism completely crystallized in them that has swallowed up the whole of their Essence and also that tendency to hate others which flows from it—the tendency, namely, which engenders all those*

---

[158] *The Tales, Ch XLVII. The Inevitable Result of Impartial Mentation, p1182*

*mutual relationships existing there, which serve as the chief cause of all their abnormalities unbecoming to three-brained beings and maleficent for them themselves and for the whole of the Universe."*[159]

This final piece of advice from Beelzebub may surprise the first time reader. But perhaps the attentive reader will not be so surprised by it. The idea was hinted at a little earlier when Beelzebub pointed out that the influence of Kundabuffer declines in old age, when the inevitability of death becomes undeniable.

If implemented, Beelzebub's idea would bring that realization forward. It would focus men's minds on the transient nature of their mundane lives and the urgent need to seek the truth about themselves and their place in the Universe.

They would better appreciate *The Terror of The Situation*.

## The Kundabuffer Narrative

The Earth was with child, and the fetus was known as Moon. It pleased the Sun and brought joy to all the planets. Moon, growing and soon-to-be-born needed to be nourished and nurtured.

Great Nature, Gaia herself, rose to the occasion. She sowed the restless oceans with plankton and populated them with fish of every imaginable size. She adorned the continents with fungi, flowers and trees. Among them, crawled mollusks, insects, and reptiles.

In their wake came kingdoms of animals and birds. And the crowning of this living and breathing world was Man, a genuine three-brained being. Surely he would become the gardener of the planet, and yearn to be among the stars from whence he came. He would search for truth within himself and in the boundless cosmos that surrounded him.

But the higher powers were concerned.

The Earth had given of itself to bestow upon Moon an inner core and a rocky surface. One and two-brained beings provided some of the substances for its atmosphere, but if Moon was to develop prop-

---

[159] *The Tales, Ch XLVII. The Inevitable Result of Impartial Mentation, p1183*

erly then Man was required to provide those higher substances, the Sacred Askokin, that can only be harvested from three-brained beings.

But would men agree to be farmed like sheep? Perhaps they would prefer to kill themselves than live in such slavery?

With permission from above, an angel from a specially convened angelic commission, implanted an organ in Man that would prevent him from ever realizing his true situation - ensuring that Moon was fed in its early fetal years and that the harmony within the solar system was not disrupted.

This was Kundabuffer, an organ at the base of the spine, which covered man's perception of reality with a veil and confused his psyche.

And when the angelic commission was convinced that harmony had prevailed, with as much grace as it could muster, it eradicated Kundabuffer entirely.

But not entirely!

The laws of the psyche are immutable.

What repeats, and repeats, and repeats in the pysche, eventually crystallizes in the psyche.

And so it was with Kundabuffer. Kundabuffer was gone but the consequences of the properties of that sorry organ remained.

The consequences were multifold. They plumbed the depths of irrationality, they explored the terrain of abject cruelty, and they thrust men into a wilderness of dreams and nightmares. And as the centuries rolled by, greater and greater numbers of these three-brained beings failed to establish their individuality.

They were transformed into machines: well-programmed robots and mindless meat puppets.

None of these consequences of the organ Kundabuffer were helpful to those three-brained beings who sought the upward path.

There was rarely any harmony.

The brutal wars – man's frequent bouts of reciprocal destruction – were dismally repetitive. They varied only in the particular area of the planet to which they laid waste. Egotistical leaders pursued power, fortune and fame and all of the other glittering prizes that Kundabuffer had burned into the suggestible mind of man.

And throngs of brainwashed meat puppets cheered them on.

At the highest level, we're told, the Absolute himself, in his sorrow, witnessed the fall of man.

How could he not know?

And when mankind had slipped too far he sent his messengers to enter the world of Man in person and, once they understood what men had become, to sound an octave of redemption and guide it by their own example.

Appearing unexpected in Moscow in the early years of the 20th century, a man called Gurdjieff brought a teaching, a beautiful and convincing revelation of the psychological world of man.

He brought objective dance, accompanied by beautiful music of his own composition. He taught men how to work consciously together in groups. He taught a new kind of science – one that paid no homage to the bristling egos of academia.

In the years that followed, as Man stumbled into the so-called Space Age, it gradually became clear that the Ray of Creation was not some meaningless mystical schematic, but the foundation stone of a new science. As the 21st century progressed data began to accumulate to flesh out the objective science that Gurdjieff gave to mankind.

So, scientific measurements now confirm that there is indeed a flow of substances from the surface of the Earth to the ionosphere, and then further. It is currently deemed to be a flow of negative ions, but from the perspective of the Work, it includes energetic substances freed at the death of one, two and three-brained beings.

And there is indeed a plasma mechanism within the Earth's magnetosphere that can, and it seems does, convey sacred Askokin to the Moon. As Gurdjieff described it, the Moon is a great electromagnet that, among other things, draws in the fragmented pieces of the false personalities and personalities of the dead, for the sake of nourishing its own nascent atmosphere.

Gurdjieff invented a new kind of literature and christened it with a timeless masterpiece. Within it, he tells the story of Kundabuffer: how and why it came to be – an unnecessary mistake by beings at a higher level than man.

More important than anything else he explains to his readers what they can do to eradicate its influence forever.

He champions being-parktdolg-duty, conscious labors and intentional suffering, which can be practiced daily.

Through the Legominism of the Holy Ashiata Shiemash, he fully describes our situation and the possibilities of reviving our buried conscience.

In particular the Five Obligolnian strivings are central to this individual effort.

Finally, from the mouth of Beelzebub, he proclaims our need to be fully and urgently aware of our own mortality.

This is The Work, for those who are willing to live it.

It offers a possibility for those who seek to escape the chains of Kundabuffer.

Man is called upon to choose:

*An eye for an eye, a tooth for a tooth and a life for a life.*

*An eye that sees for an eye that is blind,*
*A wisdom tooth for a grinding tooth,*
*A life that is lived for a life of shadows.*

# Acknowledgments

This book was edited by Paula Schmidt, without whom its readability, punctuation and production quality would be sorely deficient. Her editing skills are exceptional.

It's content is to some degree influenced by three specific study groups that devote their energies to studying *The Tales*, all of which are led by Robin Bloor. It could be said that all three of these groups made contributions. Two of these groups meet regularly on Wednesdays, the European group and the US group. The third, the Monday Group, is carried which our under the auspices of the Church of Conscious Harmony, Austin, Texas.

# Biographical Notes

Robin Bloor was born in 1951 in Liverpool, UK. He obtained a BSc in Mathematics at Nottingham University and took up a career in the computer industry, initially writing software, and eventually becoming a consultant, author and blogger. He currently resides in and works from Austin, Texas in the USA.

In 1988, Bloor met and became a pupil of Rina Hands. Rina was a one-time associate of J. G. Bennett, a student of Peter Ouspensky's, and later, a pupil of George Gurdjieff. She led groups both in London, where she lived, and in Bradford in the North of England—initially in conjunction with Rosemary Nott. She was an outstanding movements teacher and an inspirational group leader. She died in 1994 and is buried next to Jane Heap in a cemetery in North London.

Bloor leads a regular group, The Austin Gurdjieff Society, in Austin, Texas. (see ToFathomTheGist.com for details) He produces a monthly newsletter, The Lost Herald and runs the website, ToFathomTheGist.com. He also organizes multiple on-line study groups to study Gurdjieff's writings and Gurdjieff's Objective Science (as articulated by Ouspensky in *In Search of The Miraculous*, and by Gurdjieff himself in *The Tales*).

Bloor has written or edited nine books about the Work, including the present volume. Details of his other books and other books from the Karnak Press are provided on the following pages.

## To Fathom The Gist

Volume 1: Approaches to the writings of G.I. Gurdjieff
Volume II: The Arch-Absurd
Volume III: The Arousing of Thought

Rather than presenting a compendium of thoughts and theories on the meaning of *The Tales*, these books provide a practical guide on how to approach Gurdjieff's masterpiece productively. They provide clear and concise description, with abundant examples, of the approaches and techniques the reader needs to employ to better understand it.

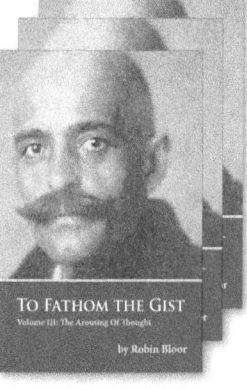

## The 1931 Manuscript (Original or Revised)

This is an edited version of the original 1931 manuscript of *Beelzebub's Tales to His Grandson*. The text is, for the most part, unchanged from the original manuscript that was published in a limited edition in 1931 by A. R. Orage. The Karnak Press published two versions of the book, both of which are available. In the original Gurdjieff's neologisms are changed to match the words in the later 1950 published version of this classic literary work, in the revised version they remain unchanged.

## The Herald of Coming Good [with notes]

Published in 1933, as a prelude to All and Everything, The Herald was written in the obtuse and difficult style of Beelzebub's Tales to His Grandson. As such, it is a mysterious publication. It pretends to be a marketing vehicle for attracting people to the Work, with registration blanks for readers to fill in – should they wish to subscribe to the books of the First Series. The casual reader is unlikely to make much sense of it, but serious readers of Gurdjieff's writings may find its contents valuable. This version of the book has been "translated" into American English and includes a rendering of the prospectus for Gurdjieff's Institute for the Harmonious Development of Man. It also includes notes on the text by Bloor.

## GURDJIEFF'S HYDROGENS
### Vol 1: The Ray of Creation

The natural companion volume to *In Search of the Miraculous by Peter Ouspensky*. This book explores the principles of Objective Science and explains why it cannot be reconciled with modern science in its current form. It then proceeds to provide a clear description of the fundamentals of Objective Science, beginning with the Ray of Creation, The Law of Seven and The Law of Three. It explains the Hydrogens and how are they derived, and then focuses on the Diagram of Everything Living, starting at its lowest point and climbing to its highest level. It examines the Trogoautoegocrat in detail and investigates the whole area of plasma and the electrical nature of life from the cell to the cosmos.

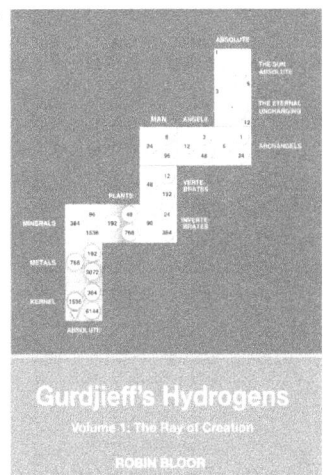

## READINGS PROSAIC AND POETIC
### Edited by R Bloor and P Schmidt

This is a selection of 108 readings that have at one time or another been read out at Gurdjieff Group meetings in the US and the UK, chosen primarily because they have an impact both on the reader and the listener.

The book includes readings from: Keats, Dostoyevsky, Jalal ad-Dīn Rumi, Schopenhauer, Lao Tzu, Marcus Aurelius, Rilke, Gurdjieff, John Bunyan, Walt Whitman, St Francis, Avicenna, Pushkin, Balzac, Milton, Rimbaud, St Paul, Blake, Shakespeare, The Bible, Li Po, Tacitus, Kirkegaard, Farid ud-Din Attar, Taylor Coleridge, Shelley, Alfred Lord Tennyson, René Daumal, Chuang Tzu, Omar Khayyam, Shelley, Turgenev, W B Yeats and many others.

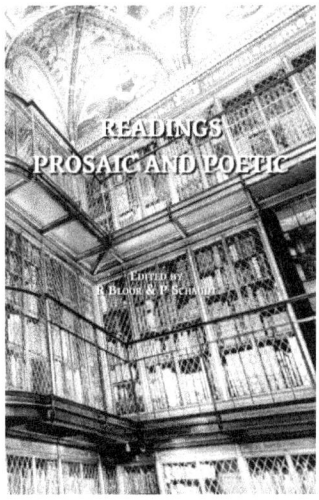

## SAYINGS FROM THE GURDJIEFF WORK
## BY ROBIN BLOOR

In this book, you'll find a wide range of quotations that cover a variety of topics, including self-knowledge, consciousness, how to approach The Work, aspects of Gurdjieff's objective science, and the meaning of man's existence. Each quotation has been carefully selected for its clarity, depth, and ability to inspire readers to reflect on their own lives and their personal work. Aside from Gurdjieff, there are chapters of aphorisms, sayings and epigrams from A. R. Orage, C. S. Nott, P.D. Ouspensky, Jeanne de Salzmann, Maurice Nicoll, Jane Heap and Rodney Collin. It also includes quotations from the writings of A. L. Staveley, Rina Hands, Katheryn Hulme, Louise March, Henri Tracol, Henriette Lannes, J G Bennet and Michel Conge.

SAYINGS FROM
THE GURDJIEFF WORK

ROBIN BLOOR

—ᴟᴟ—

## RODNEY COLLIN
## BY TERJE TONNE

. A dedicated pupil of the renowned mystic Peter Ouspensky, Collin's unique contribution to the Gurdjieff Work has had a lasting impact. Nevertheless, little is known about his early life, the time he spent with Ouspensky, and his group work - up to his mysterious death in Cuzco, Peru, at the young age of 47.

This ground-breaking biography provides a wealth of such information, most of it previously unpublished, including his close relationship to Ouspensky and a detailed account of the activities and events leading up to Ouspensky's death. It proceeds to describe the years that followed, Collin's migration to Mexico and his group activities there - also his extensive search for historical traces of The Work and his various other books and pamphlets.

RODNEY
COLLIN

## Sacred Dances - The Gurdjieff Movements
## by Nella Liska

Nella Liska provides an in-depth discussion and exploration of the Gurdjieff Movements. The book will be particularly appreciated by Movements Teachers, but will also serve as a comprehensive guide to any Movements pupil. The book covers every aspect of the Movements with chapters on: Creation and Execution, A Three Centered Approach, Clothing, Positions and Exactness,
The author draws on her decades of experience as a Movements teacher, providing insights and guidance based on her own practice and teaching, and what she has been taught by others, including all the Movement teachers who were involved in establishing the Movements in North America.

## The Search For Meaning
## by Stephen Aronson

This book examines the burning existential questions of meaning and the mystery of consciousness from a scientific and psychological perspective, through the eyes of a seasoned psychotherapist, who has long been involved in the Gurdjieff Work. It does not have the character of scientific discourse-it is more a personal odyssey through the author's world, stretching back to his earliest years, spanning his professional career and dipping into the recent events of his life. It is peppered with compelling personal experiences, psychological insights and spiritual discoveries. In his words, "Moving in this direction can lead to an experience of oneself as part of the Universe, and the Universe as a reflection of oneself.